HALLUC   S

LIFE IN THE POSTMODERN CITY

Elizabeth Wilson

RADIUS

An imprint of Century Hutchinson Ltd

An imprint of Century Hutchinson Ltd
62–65 Chandos Place, London WC2N 4NW

Century Hutchinson Australia Pty Ltd
PO Box 496, 16–22 Church Street, Hawthorn,
Victoria 3122, Australia

Century Hutchinson New Zealand Ltd
PO Box 40–086, Glenfield, Auckland 10
New Zealand

Century Hutchinson South Africa (Pty) Ltd
PO Box 337, Bergvlei 2012, South Africa

First published by Radius 1988

© Elizabeth Wilson

Set in 11/12pt Garamond Roman
By Unwin Bros. Ltd.

Printed and bound in Great Britain by
Richard Clay Ltd, Bungay, Suffolk

British Library Cataloguing in Publication Data

Wilson, Elizabeth, *1936–*
    Hallucinations: life in the post modern
    city.
    1. Great Britain. Cities. Social life
    I. Title
    941'.009'732

    ISBN 0–09–172980–7

As I was walking, one hot summer afternoon, through the deserted streets of a provincial town in Italy, which was unknown to me, I found myself in a quarter of whose character I could not long remain in doubt. Nothing but painted women were to be seen at the windows of the small houses, and I hastened to leave the narrow street at the next turning. But after having wandered about for a time without enquiring my way I suddenly found myself back in the same street, where my presence was now beginning to excite attention. I hurried away once more, only to arrive by another detour at the same place yet a third time. Now, however, a feeling overcame me which I can only describe as uncanny . . .

Sigmund Freud: 'The Uncanny'

Contents

Acknowledgements

A different version of 'Memoirs of an Anti-Heroine' appears in *Radical Records: Thirty Years of Lesbian and Gay History*, edited by Bob Cant and Susan Hemmings and published by Routledge; 'Shopping' appeared in the *Guardian*, 2 August 1986; 'Living Dolls' appeared in *Anglistica*, published by the University of Naples, and in *Linea D'Ombra*; 'Ariadne's Afternoon' appeared in *Women's Review* number 3; 'How Much is it Worth?' appeared in *Red Rag* number 10; and another version of 'Utopian Identities' appears in *Sweet Dreams*, edited by Susannah Radstone and published by Lawrence & Wishart.

1

Memoirs of an Anti-Heroine

'Hysterics suffer mainly from reminiscences.'

Sigmund Freud

These days I seldom take the road that runs along the top of Regent's Park between Camden Town and Maida Vale. But whenever I do, the ghost of a former self waits to greet me. She stands on a corner in the hysteric gaiety of a striped trouser suit and a fuchsia hat whose floppy brim shadows a deadpan face with black-circled eyes and beige lips: a fellow-traveller who lived in a different London. For if you have lived in a great city for any length of time, a slightly altered geography of streets comes to map one period onto another, so that to wander unexpectedly into some once familiar district is to walk back suddenly into the past. 'Love is here and now you're gone' – it's that romantic.

'Now is past' wrote the poet John Clare, and it is almost uncanny, the sense of actually being there, *in* that past, and yet not in it, for everything has changed. And as I lift my hand in greeting to the ghost in the striped trouser suit, her blind returning stare shows no sign of recognition: my double, she turns away, she's gone, it's the sincerest form of unrequited love, nostalgia for a former self.

'Love is here and now you're gone,' moaned the Supremes, and that was what concerned me. The attempt to have open relationships, not to be bound by heterosexual norms, led to the cul-de-sac of romantic love, work abandoned, desperate afternoons in bed, meetings in Soho

1

cafés, a walk in a wintry park, train journeys intense with longing which ended in offhand meetings in the indifferent, drab crowds in the cathedral of a railway terminus.

I had an affair with another woman. She hung out with a crowd – a married couple, both gay, they were the centre of it, and it was they who had a flat off that road that runs north of Regent's Park. They held parties – hectic scenes of rivalry were played out in a room with black walls. He played the harpsichord and told the Tarot cards with obsessional and compelling attention to detail. She told wild stories about her life and used to get picked up in the British Museum Reading Room. (After all these years I'm still chagrined that no other reader has ever tried to get off with *me*.) There was a coterie of friends – we spent a lot of time driving to one another's flats and to the Gateways Club in Chelsea.

A year or so earlier I'd been in pursuit of another woman in the group. I used to cross London on the tube to Maida Vale to see her. Once, as I waited at the interchange at Baker Street a man sidled up to me and embarked on a conversation about my schooldays. My mind on my romance, I was only half listening as gradually he worked the discussion round to school discipline, corporal punishment and caning. And it was only when he asked me if the teachers pulled my knickers down that I retreated in appalled embarrassment from this unseemly monologue, almost guilty because I felt that I must somehow have colluded, that it must have been more than absent-mindedness, some unconscious propensity of my own, even, that had permitted him to say such things. As it was, I moved off in a flustered huff, but he followed me as I boarded the train, and I remained stickily aware of his meaningful, conniving gaze from the other side of the carriage until I thankfully escaped at Warwick Avenue.

On another occasion I took a cab home from the Gateways, on my own. This time the driver's friendly small talk began with a discussion of fancy-dress parties and ended with a desperate plea for used underwear.

I did not take offence at these slightly mad, obsessed encounters, did not think of them as the intrusion of a hateful masculine sexuality, as a form of verbal sexual assault, as male violence. These fantasies which burst out into the public domain, a shared secret, yet acknowledged in public, a form of verbal flashing, marked the parameters of that 'freed' sexuality of the period, a period in which sex and madness lay close together and in which a new romanticism of lust and deviance replaced the old romanticism of adultery and the forbidden – or, as in my case, coexisted with it. I was a lesbian, a deviant also; were they not my brothers, mirror images of me, outlaws like me?

Already in the 1950s a vogue for Jacobean tragedy had foreshadowed this attraction towards a rawer, uglier sex. That strange group of plays, written in a few years around 1600 – at the very beginning of the modern period – did indeed seem modern, filled with psychopathic violence and deviant desires. Incest was one favourite theme, but most 'modern' of all perhaps, most in tune with the sixties decade, was Thomas Middleton's *The Changeling*. The giddy heroine's initial loathing of but gradual enthrallment to her disfigured servant, the repulsive de Flores, prefigured the sinister side of modern love, and could be relived in contemporary themes of the compulsion of ugliness and pornography. It might be, after all, that Beauty really loved the Beast and not the Prince.

So these phantom longings spoken by strangers, squalid in one way, or amusing as I chose to anecdotalize them, in another way spoke for the times, when to dare to speak the unprintable was to break taboos. The sixties was all about showing, displaying, saying it, as much as about doing it.

Perhaps of all the slogans of the early seventies, the gay slogan 'We are the people our parents warned us against' spoke most urgently to me. For that was what I was doing in the sixties: from the moment I first gingerly descended the stairs of the Gateways Club in 1960 to the strains of Elvis Presley's 'Only the Lonely' to my final row with the bouncer exactly ten years later, when I got banned for distributing Gay Liberation leaflets – all that time I was trying to be one of the people my mother had warned me against. Any chance encounter, therefore, that ran against the norms of bourgeois discourse, and particularly any that ran against the prescribed role for women, was to be welcomed. These men who spoke their desires might seem repulsive or comic; but at the same time, bearers of inadmissable longings to which they nevertheless frankly owned up, they appeared as witnesses, like myself, to a deeper and perhaps uglier truth than the truth of the public world above the labyrinthine map I was trying to explore. These, and other ambiguous encounters as I roamed the city, proved that I had deviated from the path of respect-ability, that I had crossed some border line. So my sixties London was not just a different geographical location, but was rather a different mental state, a geological map, a layered territory, a zone beneath – in which rules were abrogated and anything could happen, the underside of the respectable world, the world of social work to which my daily nine-to-five life was manacled.

How did I stand it for so long – that double life I led, the reluctant social worker by day, confined to a moral universe of whose values I was suspicious, who, through the looking-glass, became her mirror image, the deviant, the person she was supposed to help, by night. Actually, I needed both, needed the jarring contrasts, the moral order against which to rebel, needed the madness controlled in the hospitals and clinics where I worked *because* it roamed the streets. And I alone knew both. What would the other social workers have made of my forays to the Gateways Club? What would the women there have made of the Freudian world I lived in by day? What would Freud have made of them?

There were tough working-class women in men's suits and collars and ties, and their girlfriends in high heels, there were bohemians, boyish artists, androgynous beauties, writers, painters, poseurs, voyeurs, drunkards, and women just trying to create a space for themselves, to have a good time. Yet it was a world turned upside-down, and we who ventured into it inhabited a space between the ordinary, everyday world of the street above and an underworld that bordered at its further limits on drugs, prostitution. There, just beyond my experience it lay, a

4

MEMOIRS OF AN ANTI-HEROINE

world really beyond the pale, which I observed with interest but never let get too close to me.

Years later, though, it did brush close, but through the politics of the early seventies. For, when I was one day sitting in the Holloway Prison waiting room, due to visit an alleged member of the Angry Brigade, it was no surprise to recognize two Gateways women. The gossip had always been that they were strippers. With their blonde mink, bleached hair and pale boots as soft as kid gloves, they stood out in the shabby crowd and the cigarette smoke. I thought I'd left the apolitical years of the Gateways far behind, but here was proof that the links were closer than I'd known, that the past returns in unexpected forms, that fresh starts are never so easily made.

The sense of a decade doesn't necessarily match the actual dates, and in any case it's chance that my years at the Gateways happened to coincide exactly with the sixties. And the 'Gates' wasn't really a very sixties place – more late forties or early fifties, a drinking club in a slight time-warp, left over from an earlier bohemia.

But then what is all this about 'The Fifties', 'The Sixties' – creations of the nostalgia of the 1980s. There they are, wrapped in their separate packaging, we know all about them; and they're different, from each other as well as from us. There is the fifties, with hour-glass women back in the home, the Cold War, and weird chairs with spindly legs, with modernity and 'streamlining' in design harnessed to the imprisonment of women, with the Festival of Britain, Marilyn Monroe, Teddy boys and Harold Macmillan all jammed together; and here is the sixties, with the Pill and sexual liberation and drugs and student protest, a cocktail of Andy Warhol, the Beatles and Mary Quant shaken into a flavour of the decade.

But it was not like that at all. Today, if the fifties has become a 'lost object of desire' – an idealized representation of an in any case mythical past – then the sixties must represent for the collective psyche an awakening to hedonism, politics and decadence that is also partly fictional; not another utopia, perhaps, more a romanticized hell, the years of licence. Sometimes the optimism of either

5

or both is set against the cynicism of today, iron times against a golden age. At the time it all seemed different, and, of course, more confused, and there was a whole period when the fifties and sixties were both happening at once – say from 1956 to 1964, which had the flavour of both.

And even before that it was such a world of double vision, the double vision that nostalgia always seems to lose in its search for the essence of time. 1953, for example: there's the Coronation, a pastiche enactment of the medieval with heraldic animals made of plaster, regalia red lipstick, and necking in front of the television as we watch the blue and white images jerk by, how does she go to the lavatory we wonder, as Richard Dimbleby intones. There's a surfeit of spectacle and boredom.

Later, across the Atlantic is that other enthronement, the gruesome Other (yet horribly concealed) spectacle of a woman enthroned, as Ethel Rosenberg steps up to the electric chair – those photographs in the papers, when they were arrested, faces white and pasty in the flash-bulb light, a suppressed horror behind those smeared images, now, after years of waiting, fulfilled in that ultimate room, the room with the electric chair. How could they do that to anyone? But they did. So there's the Queen on her throne, just an ordinary young woman, a real person, yet framed in the cardboard pomp of fake medievalism; and there's that room, posing as an ordinary room, with an ordinary chair in the middle, site of a ritual so horrible that you're not allowed to see. Only all the lights flickered in the stifling town and there was smoke from the chimneys.

So then, 1956, and that time between, as the leaden clouds of cold war began to lift and life opened out, protest began. 'Kinky' was an in word by 1961, yet those years seemed to have a freshness, an innocence that was lost in the later sixties. More innocent than the fifties by far. The fifties had been so sinful, so *old*. In my twenty-first birthday photograph my dark lips, vaselined lids, tightly waved hair, stiff black dress and pearl necklace age me poignantly; but by the time I reach thirty I'm dressed like a Kate Greenaway child in white stockings, flat shoes and high-waisted dresses, with my cropped hair I look about twelve years old. There must have been a dislocation in travelling backwards so fast, so far.

That dark adulthood of adolescence in the fifties, when love was important and serious, and we looked for a meaning in life through poetry and religion and passion; the metaphysical poets with their seventeenth-century 'modern' imagery and their longings, loneliness and guilt, a portent of my twentieth-century soul, said it all. But it wasn't just in poetry, it was in pop as well – 'Night Riders in the Sky', about being in love and dying young.

When the Profumo affair seethed to the surface it brought everything about the fifties and the sixties together, on the cusp of 1963. The Profumo affair was neither quite of the fifties nor of the sixties, or rather, it partook of both: the end of the repressed, drinking-club, sex-for-hire world of fifties bohemia (to which the Gateways also belonged), where even adultery could take you close to the margins; and the beginning of the satirical sixties, the iconoclasm and end to deference. Yet the darkness continued, for the assassination of President Kennedy seemed to inaugurate an era of crazy murders, sometimes political, always excessive, the Moors murderers most of all – just as sixties as Jackie Kennedy – so that more and more you knew that anything could happen to anybody, no one was ever really safe.

I was hell-bent on pleasure, skating on the surface of the social whirl. Already the earnest hopefulness of the fifties was tarnished with cynicism, and, more than that, the sixties was shot through with angst and madness. The bright young things like me stood on the edge of a volcano and peered in, maybe giggling and excited, but there was horror as well. Those were the moods of the sixties, horror and excitement; infantile moods to set against the gloom and aspiration of the fifties. The desire to be grown up had gone. Others may have a different memory, but for me the childish aspects were more of the *Brideshead Revisited* kind, a far from innocent adult imitation of childhood. And by 1967 pastiche was already around: there were *Bonnie and Clyde* gangster suits, fedoras and berets; Mary

7

Quant made little crepe frocks in dirty shades of cocoa, dusty pink and prune, and you could hang out in that camp emporium, Biba's, where feather boas festooned the bentwood stands and you could buy Jean Harlow outfits of sleazy boudoir satin, the Biba face embellished Theda Bara style with sepia lipstick and ochre powder.

Now we used to go on after closing time at the Gateways to strange basements where silent movies flickered along the walls and crowds decked in portable outrage openly smoked joints. The Supremes and Dusty Springfield sang romance at the Gateways still, but the rock music in these new dungeons went way beyond that sentimental sense of loss; love like drowning in a sea of music became love like porn, raw nerves and hatred, hard images that mocked romantic love. The anarchy of sex could be a way of breaking the back of society: 'Sex is the only way to infuriate them. Much more fucking and they'll be screaming hysterics in next to no time.'[1]

The opening out of sexuality that occurred, though, was it ever more than the inverse of the romantic, tight-arse fifties? A confusion of sensations, a confusion of being, a sense of things boiling up, a great froth of sinister energy bubbling into the culture, spreading across its surface, and the people your parents had warned you against appeared through the smoke and the strobe lights with all the tacky drama of a drag queen.

Yet what it was all about was always the search for authenticity. In the fifties authenticity meant truth to feelings, truth to one's own individuality. In the sixties it was the same, only the means to unearthing that truth had somehow changed. For subjectivity was substituted excess, no longer the mind's barriers that had to be crossed, but the body's; instead of metaphysical poets and existentialism it was the deadpan joke of pop art and the unmasking of society's lie, the lie of culture, the lie of power, the lie of fine feelings. It was the time of unmasking when the mad and the stoned were the vessels of truth, yet it was also the time of masks and disguises.

It wasn't that it was really any crazier than the fifties, because part of what makes modernity modern is the current of madness that is always there; woven into its fabric the warp of madness, the beauty of excess blends with the poison of a normality that is always phony. It was only that in the sixties the madness took a new and less lugubrious form.

It was crazy in another way too, crazy with money. As the real boom ended, we got to hear about the boom, the money seemed to flow faster, you could buy things you'd never dreamt of before, shopping was the flavour of the decade. You needed shopping in order to construct your Image, your disguise, you needed shopping and the media. From that marriage came Image, religion of style. *Queen* magazine was my bible; look through those sixties back numbers now and it might be today, it's so much the same, from the spaghetti-strap underslip dresses to the obsession with names and style and the way-of-the-world knowing-ness and the way that politics is mixed in with night-club gossip.

'Whaddya want if ya don't want money, whaddya want if ya don't want love?' crooned Adam Faith at the turn of the decade. Authenticity? The authenticity of the fifties had been innocent – even in searching for the truth through self-knowledge of one's own iniquity, guilt and excess: the spies and the traitors, the homosexuality, the middle-class Christians, it was all the same thing, was all about redemption. But in the sixties we were crazy with relief because we'd discovered that it wasn't our fault after all, it was the culture that was corrupt, and so rebellion and politics was the answer, there was nothing to redeem, it was right to rebel.

I think the Tories have got it all wrong about the sixties. They shouldn't blame the sixties. They should be grateful – for the fermenting individualism, for the crazy joy of the consumer world, for the lust for love and money, for the surreal dress rehearsal (of cultural happenings and art protest) for the real thing of now.

Yet there was a difference. Then, the social 'discoveries' – of poverty, of homelessness, of loneliness, of cruelty – came as a shock. Now, on the other hand, everyone *knows*, but the underside of affluence, the underclass in its picturesque squalor of Merseyside sink estates and romantic junkiedom becomes merely an ironic backdrop for the consumerism of the eighties, it's actually an essential part of the spectacle, no deeper truth but merely another appearance.

And similarly I could not be today what I thought I was then: an anti-heroine, a deviant, an outsider. Today there are no rebels, only pariahs; no outsiders, only unbeings; no revolutionaries, only 'proles'. Then, lesbianism was elevated into an interesting, if flawed, moral condition; today lesbians and gays are simply less than human – although at a level of privilege journalists can write about 'designer dykes' in glossy magazines as though it were just another option. It's a lifestyle those perverts *choose*. So kill them for it; kill them for a matter of style.

Then, sex with women wasn't 'real' sex, love with women, in the words of one of the many psychoanalysts with whom I crossed swords during those years, was 'more than love, but really less than love'. Our nostalgia for that past, too, is 'more than love, but really less than love'. Already then, in the sixties, nostalgia for the thirties, nostalgia for the forties clung to our sensibility with its own brand of claustrophobic longing. Nostalgia evades confusion, in its veiled vision of the past all is acceptable, we are robbed of indignation, trade it in for a depoliticized imagery in which both privilege and poverty, and oppression itself are merely picturesque.

2

Gossiping Days

The texture of a great city; it has a four-dimensional quality – for years you can live in the next street to an old lover, a once close friend, and not even know it, your pathways cross to and fro, interweaving invisibly, lives plotting their course, similar lives, although they always felt so different, it's not surprising you've ended up in the same postal district even if you split up years ago or simply drifted apart, or were only throw together in the first place through the accident of work or mutual friends. Through the drifting crowds the threads weave in and out, day after day, year after year; and if you knew, if you were aware of that pattern forming you'd realize how little you were in command, and that while you experience each choice as both a responsibility and a source of pride, an affirmation of uniqueness ('We're moving!'; 'I've got a new job!') it's always already determined. Everyone's doing the same thing, the pattern forms, the threads weave in and out, it goes forward all the time, you can never stop, never unpick.

So: I moved twenty minutes to the west and crossed a borough boundary. It seemed momentous.

Just off the main road at the top of our street, if you turn left there's a little garden. You'd never notice it, the alleyway that runs up the back, between the houses, is hidden, overgrown with shrubs and trailing ivy, part of the city's secret grid, the underside of the city, loose threads, the city unravelling in its tangle of gardens and pathways and wasteland behind the neat facades, the undress of the city you see from the little North London line train.

11

HALLUCINATIONS

When Peaches the toddler was with her childminder I used to collect her and take her up there, on the way home, in the warm September afternoons. The garden was circular, hollowed out of the hedges and surrounding walls, wih three entrances from different sides; so you could walk home a different way, through the flats and across the road by the Armenian cobbler and the second-hand clothes shop.

There were swings and a slide and a climbing structure made of split logs and heavy metal. But it was more or less empty at that time, at tea-time. A mother with a new baby in a pram might be seated on one of the benches under the lime trees in the far corner, an old man with a stick might contemplate the bees that seemed to slumber on the wing above the few late flowers, there'd be a cluster of children, their light voices lost in the still air. The gold bars of sunlight weighed heavily on us all, an amber afternoon.

I pushed the swing forward and back, forward and back. When the woman – materialized; she was suddenly there behind me. I hadn't seen her enter the enclosure, walk across the grass.

She said my name at the same moment as I saw her. She hadn't changed at all, I'd have recognized her anywhere. A beautiful face with elongated blue eyes, long nose, wide cheekbones, wide mouth and a soft, sly Scottish touch to her voice; it was still there, still in place. It was the smile most of all; her smile extended this instant friendship and warmth, enveloped you.

Her hair was lighter now, and shorter. Long and black, it had given her a slightly witchlike quality in 1965. Then, there'd been an atmosphere of drama, her nose had been spikier, her eyes wilder, there were love affairs, days missed from work, altercations with the boss, Paris weekends from which she'd failed to return. I'd liked her then, but had steered clear. Now – a pang of regret that I'd never tried to be friends, had enjoyed but been scared of her gossipy malice, her tales and dramas, her cackle of laughter. She'd had a nose for what was going on, but I'd shielded myself, had wanted her not to know anything about my dramas,

12

hadn't wanted my angst-ridden love affairs reduced to a caricatured anecdote. Twenty years too late that seemed a mistake, and I wished I'd had her salty laughter to wash the wounds, stinging but salutary, she'd have seen the funny side of it all, and then I'd have had to too.

Her children, two long-haired girls, soar on the swings. You can see it's all come right for her, the wonderful clothes, a dress with Liberty flowers in cream and pink on indigo, and Italian shoes in cranberry leather, and, yes, she tells me all about it as we stand by the swings. She's a therapist now, her husband's a consultant, it all fits in with the children, they like her to be at home when they come out of school –

And what's so amazing is the way she's kept up with everyone; I myself hardly need to tell her my news, she's heard about it somehow. She's kept up with all of them, colleagues I'd never have thought to see or hear of again, she's involved, lives in the present, has an appetite for human contact, so that the past feeds, nourishes the present, whereas with me they're kept strenuously apart, don't I fling my past away, and yet it hangs about and drains the present –

So we talk about the gossip of long ago, of the tragic love affairs of those two, the couple we knew at that clinic long ago. They were both married. He was a Catholic and argued passionately about something called the Natural Law, while his wife lay at home and had miscarriage after miscarriage. The woman was older than he was, and her husband much older again, a rich man, part of that stuffy, old-fashioned, provincial business community, a family out of a middlebrow novel, a tale of provincial life. Things were different then, divorce was still difficult; but they made the break, fought their way out of duty, snatched at love.

Only then – he was killed in an accident, just like that, from one day to the next. And not long afterwards she had a heart attack, quite a young woman really, but they said she had no will to live, no will to recover, she died, really, of grief. All that for nothing, the divorces, the guilt, the pain. For love; a few months of love.

13

Our boss disapproved. And now we gang up on him; what a pig the man was: Harvey – that was his name.

'Didn't you go to Paris one weekend, and when you got back late he tried to have you fired –?'

'He told me I wasn't to wear a skirt and blouse to the office, it had to be a suit or dress and jacket –'

'He absolutely *hated* women –'

'Oh yes, that was *crystal* clear –'

'So obsessional, all those machines and gadgets –'

'His *pipe*. I *hated* the way he fiddled with it –'

I wonder what's happened to him, retired by now perhaps, but even she doesn't know. It's time to go home, but we linger there. There begins to be a slight sharpness in the air, it's softened to grey beneath the trees, the sun's sunk down behind the wall of houses, the call of the children sounds like birds. The ripe languor of the afternoon has a plangent note, a blue note.

Softly, warmly we part, without saying goodbye, almost conspiratorial, that sympathy between women bathes us momentarily, you might almost call it indulgence, we'd forgive each other anything, we forgive those crass, silly, immature selves.

We'll meet again, two ghosts from the past.

One afternoon I'm working at home when there's a caller. She's come to consult my friend on a union matter, but my friend is late, as usual. I therefore have tea with this vivacious, grey-haired woman, who wears a gingham dress and simple sandals. She has a small head on a graceful neck and slants her gaze from side to side as elegant and smiling as a Burmese cat. We talk about cats and gardens.

My friend comes home and I go upstairs again. Only something haunts me, there's something familiar –

It is, it's Victoria, we were in the sixth form together. I haven't seen her from that day to this, but she hasn't really changed. Then, she was the daring one, a string of boyfriends, she didn't go to college like the rest of us, but to art school instead; it seemed rather louche at the time. She was the first girl I ever saw dressed in trousers with flies, bright green, they buttoned up over her concave

14

stomach in a most suggestive way, and she went to coffee bars and all-night parties.

I have to see if it's true.

'Oh yes,' she says, 'you were the very young one, who was clever and good at games.'

I don't remember being good at games – and was I so much younger? She speaks admiringly, but I always felt unpopular. And she was rather a snob. Her best friend was the daughter of an earl.

I was different, so different from them. But now we're living less than half a mile apart and we both work in the public sector.

There's a college-wide protest meeting, colleagues I've never even seen before. And I recognize him, seated in the crowded lecture theatre. To me he was the embodiment of brains and sophistication. He looks much the same – which means that he looks out of date in a patched tweed jacket that would have seemed bohemian when he was a student, with the black shirt and woolly beige tie. The long hair too, it's long like it was then, not the way hair is long now. I thought he was a most superior being. And now he's slogging it out in the public sector, just like me.

The first man I slept with – I thought it was Love at the time. Now it seems more like a desperate act of defiance.

We meet again, in the little garden hollowed out between the houses. Peaches staggers sickeningly along the climbing frame, I'm trying not to be terrified (how much should you let them do by themselves?), when she appears as silently as before, elegant this time in a putty-coloured mac – it's later in the autumn now – and again we talk of the past.

'You *know*,' she says, 'I've discovered that something *horrible* happened to Harvey –'

'I had a letter from Ann –'

Another friend from that far-off time – she really does keep up with them all.

'She wouldn't tell me in the letter – but I was driving through one day and stopped off to see her –'

15

She drops her voice, and there's a hint of the old drama: 'he committed *suicide* you know – '

We stare at each other: suicide. It was *that bad* then. He persecuted us, made us feel small, despised young women, patronized, trying to be fatherly, it was all so tacky – he made me talk about myself, and did an instant psychoanalytic diagnosis, afterwards I felt I'd betrayed myself, and hated him more than ever. But I remember him saying something about loneliness then.

'His wife left him, you know – '

'But she was so *dull*. He seemed embarrassed when she was around – '

'Perhaps he needed her though – '

The soft grey afternoon creeps round us. It's the dull, dead time of autumn now, the leaves lie colourless along the grass like scraps of crumpled paper.

She smiles. There's this complicity. We knew each other in a different life. And death only makes it more real, more fixed, more timeless, a world preserved in the film archives in one's head, a world that runs alongside the daily life of now, the criss-crossing of invisible acquaintances in a few square miles of streets and parks, the layers of the inner city, where past and present mingle to that thick patina of half-sad expectation.

3

Shopping

The shop is always open. All hours of the day and late into the night its air-conditioned aisles are waiting; it reminds me of the supermarket in a dusty corner of Manhattan where I hung out one year, in a heatwave –

It's never full. Down the high street, at the Superstore, the stalwart families crowd along the aisles, trolleys are stacked high with a fortnight's provisions, giant cartons of Ricicles, a kilo of frozen chips, a sack of apples, tins for the cats; the up-market types fill theirs with muesli, fresh pasta, gallons of fat-free milk, lamb's lettuce, venison and trout. There's a crush at the cabinets, jostling at the meat counter for outsize joints, a queue for hot baked bread. Children get a ride in the wheeler, or cling to their mothers' skirts, there's howling and sucking of sweets, while the older ones dart up and down with items that were forgotten, self-important on trips for paper cups and marmalade. The place is jammed with the eighty per cent at work. The car park's full, more queues to get in and out, they had to close the doors at Christmas, and now there's a new crime: steal the piled-up provisions from the boot, while the driver's gone off to park the trolley.

At the corner shop it's empty. The families never come here, the normal, nine-to-five or Saturday shoppers, the housewives, the women with baskets on wheels or a car in the parking lot. This is a shop for after hours. Begins to come to life in the early evening. Singles stop by on the way home from work, to pick up a bottle of wine and a dinner for two: an avocado, frozen steak, ice-cream and some razor blades or a new pair of tights – the hope of a

17

seduction, perhaps. Or there are the lonely diners: fish fingers, Mars bars; a tin of soup and some frozen pancakes; peanut butter and crisps – in tiny flats they indulge in strange food fads, in diets that act as unconscious gestures of defiance at absent parents.

Two teenage mothers wander in for some fags and the smallest size packet of Pampers, all they can afford at one time, on the dole. They're dressed in their oldest clothes, treat the place like their own back yard, hang out at the corner by the soap powder to have a gossip with a mate from the flats.

There's a brisk trade in Hirondelle and cans of beer all evening, as the young set out in twos and threes for a convivial evening. Late at night a district wino shambles round, prone to curse and shout. But the three young Asians at the checkout are laid back and friendly about it, they're courteous and calming, he's soothed, here even the outcast is welcomed and served like the rest.

Sunday's the busy day. A famous writer does her shopping masked with sunglasses. In the afternoon a group of punks lark about, but their needs are rather poignantly domestic – just like the rest of us they only want some Persil, teabags and bread. Two gays perch, seated sideways, on the frozen food cabinet. They're talking about love:

'It was *really heavy* – '
'I don't think you should see him again – '
'The thing is, I do quite like him – '

You can tell the lonely, they line up with a little piece of meat, a drink, a tinned roly-poly pudding for one. It's a refuge for the lonely, the forlorn, the marginal, the deviants. Only here they're revealed as domestic, unthreatening like the rest of us, buying a few small items to keep life going, or a little treat to brighten up the evening. The atmosphere's benign, softens the jagged edges of urban anonymity, inner-city fear.

Late in the evening I sidle out myself for some extra milk for Peaches the toddler, a tin of Whiskas for Coco the cat, booze for the grown-ups. One of the assistants is coming along the road towards me, and gives me a smile and a nod. I smile back, shamefaced. He recognized me! I must be a regular then, another of the sluts who can't get it together to do my shopping at the normal time, who inverts the natural order of things, no housewifely routine.

'Slut shop's busy tonight,' I announce on my return.

Our visitor is shocked. 'You shouldn't use *that word*,' she frowns. Slut: it denigrates women. I feel guilty; politically incorrect again.

'But *I'm* a slut,' I say, trying to stick up for myself.

Long ago, in the sixties, Katherine Whitehorn stunned her *Observer* audience by writing an article in which she came out as a slut. Sighs of relief and identification were expelled across thousands of AB Sunday breakfast tables at the discovery that the reader wasn't the only woman who mended her suspenders with an aspirin tablet (for this was just before the advent of tights) or pulled a dirty shirt out of the laundry basket *in order to wear it again*. At last the silence had been broken. The word, the condition was reclaimed. Now we could all admit we were sluts and strike a blow against the oppressive norms of housewifery and the feminine role.

'I *like* being a slut,' I growl, belligerent, as I used to scowl at my mother.

But our relationship to language has changed since those far-off days. Then it was just a middle-class joke, now we can no longer ignore the real hatred behind the word, the sexual innuendo, the policing of women by language.

Can 'slut' no longer be claimed as outlawry, defiance, be worn as a sign of revolt, like my white lips and beatnik hair when I scowled at my mother?

'You're right, you're right,' I mutter.

The slut shop, 'sluts' for short, to be referred to henceforth as the corner shop, strikes a blow, all the same, for those values, and in doing so recognizes the real inhabitants of this neck of the inner city: those who live after hours, without a daily routine or a nine-to-five job or a nuclear family, balancing in the interstices of urban life, tightrope-walking between crazy fun and just being crazy, down and out or having a ball, a life of violent contrasts and sudden whims or needs that the corner shop can satisfy. At five to

19

midday on a Sunday the drinkers gather outside the door, desperate they grab each passer by – can you tell us the time, it is five to, two minutes to – it's one minute to! On the dot they push each other to get in first, to grab their bottles of cider. On the door a new notice has appeared: 'We accept milk tokens.' What are they? Instead of benefit? We haven't got any.

It's not a shop for the respectable, for the rooted, but performs a social service, it's a social work office of the free market, where spending a little money can tide you over for the time being.

For a while I tried to remember to call it the corner shop, but 'sluts' has gradually crept back I'm afraid. Peaches and I stroll down on a Sunday evening. She wants a bag of crisps. It's the usual crowd. The famous writer's there incognito again; and the bikers from the flats –

Later still I have to go back. The cat wouldn't eat the Whiskas (although eight out of ten cats say they prefer it, or is it their owners – who's actually eating it, anyway) so I have to get some frozen fish. It's late. The high road's empty now. But still the nighthawks mooch around the chilly aisles, the chocolate addicts stocking up for the night, it's the Good Breast, the place that takes the waiting out of wanting.

4

City Travellers

They came at Christmas time. One day the triangular space next to the railway was empty, the next a caravan was parked there. Came in the night. Then there were two, three, five. Going home in the chilly dusk Peaches the toddler points and screams, the children are still playing among the puddles and gravel behind the wire fence. Peaches is mad to join them, she gazes with baleful longing at the tiny, busy children running between the trailers. As you pass you can see the blue square of a telly inside the nearest caravan and a woman bathing a baby in that tiny space. It's all so neat.

Before, it had been a used car lot. It was horrible then. An intercom echoed across the street all day, calling to no one. Now, tidied up, it serves a useful purpose. Three of the boys career out of a side alley, tobogganing on a trolley the fishmonger long ago abandoned. A little girl sits on the steps with bare feet, and washes her doll in a puddle.

Peaches screams to join them, she knows it's a free life beyond the wire, she bellows and strains at her pushchair every time we go past. They used to say that travellers stole children. Now I understand it was always the other way round, the children ran away to join them, couldn't wait to be off.

Not everyone shares Peaches' view. A neighbour stops me in the street.

'Milk bottles've been walking,' he informs me with a meaningful nod. 'The milkman said a whole crate of milk walked – he just went up in the flats and when he got back – gone, a whole crate.'

'Oh dear.'

'The people opposite said the *dustbins* walked.'

The dustbins waddled across the road, to run away with the gypsies. Peaches would waddle off too if she got half a chance.

The neighbour reads my silence as dissent, adds reproachfully,

'All right for us, we don't live opposite. Still, there's an eviction order now, they won't be here long.'

I imagine them having a merry Christmas on the used car lot. When we get back, they've gone. But they've only moved down the road to the blighted triangular garden under the railway arch. The local paper's full of it already: beleaguered councillors, tenants' groups up in arms. The dismal square, once a meths drinkers' haven, has suddenly become a precious local amenity, no longer just an enlarged traffic island full of dusty privet, but a treasured green space. There are more caravans. The argument surges across the Council chamber. Meanwhile the mats and carpets are taken out and aired, hung over the fence every morning, washing strung across the privets as the trains thunder across the viaduct.

Peaches doesn't notice them now, when we pass by in the bus. Everything close to her is so huge, she hasn't time for anything further away. She frowns at a yelling baby in the next seat:

'Cry-ing,' she observes, as of a recognized but alien phenomenon, remote from her personal experience.

So she doesn't notice the travellers, they've spread out now, they've begun to encroach onto the bomb site that will one day be the new Superstore Year 2000 (also focus of ferocious local battles) but which for now is the ruins of an Art Deco factory with an awesome crater a hundred feet deep at its centre. The caravans perch on the edge of this cliff, inhabiting the waste land with aplomb.

It's a hot autumn day and two of their little boys are fishing in a drain on the main road, lying flat on the pavement, treating it as if it were a river bank, the way they have of making strange the familiar, of using the taken-for-granted in an unexpected way. Is that why people hate them? They treat the urban as though it were rural, they survive the way the foxes and badgers on the railway embankment survive, they're not meant to be there, they've made things ambiguous, hedgehogs and badgers should live in the country, in the nice, tidy, sanitized, child's picture-book countryside where rabbits have names like Bigears and Fluffy.

Likewise the travellers; in books they're romantic, but here they call into question the regime of the city, they remind you of the cracks in the pavement through which the weeds will push, remind you that every city is impermanent too, only a ruin in waiting, that the encroachment of nature is kept at bay only by unceasing vigilance, and that in any case you shouldn't be lying on the river bank at all, but should be rushing from point A to point B in a fast-moving vehicle.

The travellers bring things back to some more personal scale, domesticating the underside of the city, merging public and private. They pose a different set of values – or am I only compounding the prejudice by treating them as separate, strange? The travellers found a use for that ugly little strip of land by the railway cutting. Now it's an abandoned eyesore, with mounds of earth piled round the gate to stop them from getting back.

Meanwhile they take their stand under the railway arches, and the traffic pours round them with dust and din.

5

Madonna of the High Road

Monkfish! Smoked chicks! Carp! Every Saturday she writes the good news up along the window in large white chalky letters. You gaze beyond them at the marble slab. A fish shop is different. There's a hint of zoology or the aquarium as you stare at the nacreous carp, the swordfish, the orange-tinted parrot fish (what's that!) and the bruise-coloured flesh and gaping mouth of the tuna beached across its rock of ice. The ocean seems close by. Whereas whoever thinks of an orchard when they buy a pound of golden delicious, or of a farm at the butcher's?

Beyond, *she* presides. Her hands encased in fastidious pink rubber gloves hover above the filleted kippers and freckled codling. The queue lengthens. At each of us she smiles, a sweet, sad smile, which places her immensely far above us. She is always immaculate; lipstick that matches her gloves, a perfect complexion, smooth dark hair drawn back into a ballerina chignon. At the rear of the shop there's a freezer cabinet and an arrangement of shells, and her husband sits behind. He looks ill, rests a lot, passes the time of day with a few favoured customers. She weighs up the prawns and the coley and fillets the plaice.

The man in front of me turns to the queue as her knife slips under the backbone quick as a flash.

'Look at that,' he says, 'why it's almost an art, now isn't it.'

Her faint, contemptuous smile; he's done for himself with that 'almost'. *Almost* an art: why, of *course* it's an art, to strip the flesh from the bones in thirty seconds flat and sweep the knife across the board, sending the scraps into

24

the bucket that waits at the end of the counter. A sleight of hand; you hardly saw it happen; a conjuring trick to produce two pure white tongues of flesh.

Just what Peaches the toddler likes for tea. Coco the cat gets the scraps, or a lump of coley. The coley's cheap, most of the customers buy it for themselves. They've always run out by lunchtime.

I pass by at eight in the morning, on my way to the baths for an early swim. Round the back there's a strong fishy smell, and I can see her washing down the floor at the back. She wears a big apron, and wellington boots. I suppose they've been to Billingsgate already – stink and uproar, innards, slime and blood.

She begins to arrange the display in a pattern of pale, cold colours spiked with the green of parsley. The whiting are curled with their tails in their mouths, a cornucopia of shiny black mussels spills over into the prawns and lemons, the sharpness, the rawness of it all sets your teeth on edge, and the fronds of the squid tentacles stretch like pink ferns towards the rosy wings of skate.

Her smile is fixed. She touches the fish with the tips of her gloves, drops the money in the till with a gesture of disavowal. She softens for Peaches, but with all of us she's so cool, so gracious.

'We-must-get-Coco-some-fish-for-tea,' intones Peaches on the way home.

'The queue's too long.' I lead her away. But she climbs out of the buggy and starts to run back, clings screaming to the railings along by the school. Her face turns beetroot purple.

'But I liked that fish shop, I did,' she bellows, 'I wanna go back to that fish shop, we haven't got Coco anything for tea, have we.' And then the final accusation: 'Look – now you've made me cry again, Lizzabuff.'

Again. We go back. She hiccoughs piteously in the shop, working her blotched face for all the sympathy she can get. When she finally clasps the slithery packet of fish in her hands she calms down. The fish shop's very soothing; a form of benediction.

One Sunday evening I happen to pass by. There's a dim light in the back of the shop, and I can see two men, strangers, moving around, they're arranging bottles of vinegar where the conch shells used to be. And they've moved the freezer cabinet, which used to be festooned with a fisherman's net.

On the Tuesday I go in as usual, and there they are again, in aprons and straw hats. They've smartened the place up a bit, but the display's not half as artistic. I enquire, with sinking heart.

'Oh yes, they've retired – we've taken over – but Ernestine will be back on Friday to say goodbye to all her customers –'

No more pink gloves, lifting, letting go the fish; no more world-weary smiles at the vagaries of customers; no more sprigs of parsley tucked into the cods' rictus jaws.

Goodbye Ernestine.

6

Bricolage City

◆◇

The blue sofa appeared like a vision in Frank's window, an answer to prayer – I'd been looking for months. A beautiful soft shade of blue tinged with turquoise, it had real feather pillows, solid wooden legs, it was a traditional design from the twenties I should think, probably started life in Maples. This miracle induced a sense of triumph: faith *is* rewarded after all. But then I noticed that it was in fact a three-piece suite, that two bulging armchairs squatted in the wings. It was rather as when an attractive girl hitch-hiker turns out to have two male companions lurking in the bushes.

Only £90, mind you, for the three, but had we room for those obese items, ungainly and awkward by contrast with the gloriously expansive settee. One in the basement, possibly . . . or maybe Frank would let me have the sofa on its own, suppose I offered him £90 just for the sofa – but Frank wasn't around, so I decided to sleep on it.

The new neighbours' dog howled and whined all evening. What are they *doing* to it, I ought to ring the RSPCA – and they played their record with the windows open. They only had the one: Andrew Lloyd Webber's greatest hits. Seated at my desk I was not working, but was locked in an internal dialogue as I projected myself onto their doorstep: 'I *wonder* if you'd mind –' (aristocratic, overdone politeness); 'I *am* trying to work, you know –' (aggressive self-importance); or there was the guilt-inducing angle of references to lost sleep and cruelty to animals. I did nothing. They sounded so happy, moving their furniture

27

about, running up and down the stairs, shouting at each other, banging nails into walls.

My mother used to claim that our family, by reason of its Celtic origins, enjoyed the gift of second sight. And certainly, as I approached Frank's shop, a premonition gripped me. Sure enough – it had gone. Where yesterday the blue sofa, so invitingly crumpled, had lolled, today a horrible mustard-coloured cut moquette job squared up belligerently to the window-shoppers.

Frank's mate was shifting the second-hand fridges around. "That blue sofa?' I asked, hoping against hope. His face was long and sad. "Oh, nah, that's gorn. Sold. The suite, you mean."

I turned away with that feeling you get when you've just read the letter informing you you didn't get the job, or that your lover's got married. Angry with yourself – pusillanimous again, ambivalent; you didn't *really* go for it. Couldn't make up your mind. In the street I ran into Frank himself. 'You sold the blue sofa!' (Please, oh please say I can still have it.) 'Oh yeah – I took that round to your neighbours, next door.'

I walked off stonily. Not to *them*. So that's what they were shoving around all night. Anyone else I wouldn't have minded so much . . . I hated them. All day I schemed to think how I might get it back – I'd steal it when they were away, I'd offer them £200, I'd . . .

Frank's shop is situated in the middle of a network of little streets given over to the sale of second-hand furniture, antiques and junk. There is a brisk trade in stripped-pine dressers and Victorian grates, Art Deco lamps and Clarice Cliff teasets. Frank's shop is cheaper than the others, and filled with just the sort of stuff you need when furnishing a second home. There are mattresses leaning against the walls, cookers, cupboards, armchairs, the odd hoover. How does he know where to get it? Does he read the small ads in the *Evening Argus*, or scan the death column, or go to auctions, or is there an informal network running along the coast road, informing him of impending removals and garage sales?

The recycling of possessions is what the post-industrial economy – both here and in the third world – is all about. And in this seaside city it's brought to a fine art. Further towards the London Road are all the second-hand clothes shops, filled with old ladies' fur coats and leftovers from the early seventies. The days are long gone when you could hope to find a forties suit or a thirties frock in these emporia of lost lives. Now it is long batik dresses and cheesecloth blouses, purple polyester flares and plastic shoes with square toes and heels, and the short-sleeved acrylic lacy jumpers, beige and off-white, worn only by women over sixty. There are used saucepans, electrical gadgets that no longer work and dog-eared volumes of Judith Krantz and Jeffrey Archer – a whole other (nether) world of pleasures and anxieties, of breakdown and brico-lage, of the accumulation of personalized oddments, the refuse of the consumer world, the 'Other' of the bright, smart chain stores up on Churchill Square. It all reminds me of my mother and grandmother in their house stuffed with objects of sentimental value, odd buttons in boxes, mementoes in drawers, piles of newspaper cuttings, old medals and spectacles, programmes and recipes, diaries and shoehorns, handbags, paper knives, polished Cairngorm stones, and stamps and coins no longer current but not yet valuable.

It reminds me also of the Third World Exposition in Amsterdam: visited by chance because it was a rainy afternoon. A whole section of it was devoted to the useful objects made from the detritus we throw away – oil drums, plastic containers, cardboard boxes, all transformed as tables, teapots, storage. My grandmother never threw any-thing away.

There's a whole lifestyle that goes with bricolage. The woman behind whom I stood in the queue at the Preston Road post office – she was dressed in some of those second-hand clothes – cashed her giro, then entered into a complicated transaction involving the purchase of saving stamps for gas and TV, the paying-off of another bill with a different set of stamps, the cashing of a postal order, and a request for exactly enough postage stamps for her little pile of letters.

But up on Churchill Square the high street fashions, the hair gel and the credit cards are flashing as the boutique manageresses and the junior estate agents shop through the lunch hour: a floating population, more floating than most. The two women in the teashop have money on their minds as they smear their scones and spear their chocolate cake. Their artificiality is naturalized by its familiarity: the tousled, tumbling curls have been layered, tinted and streaked; a special shade of apricot blusher, the biggest make-up cliché of them all, shadows the cheekbones, and a similar natural-unnatural shade shimmers on slightly parted lips, the edges of which each woman occasionally touches with a fingernail, scraping off a minute quantity of caked grease; their eyesockets gleam with peach and violet, fringed with cobalt blue lashes. The effect is stylized yet banal, the re-creation of faces we've seen thousands of times in magazines, the expression of vacant challenge carefully maintained; and the air of muted sexual provocation emphasized by the pink and turquoise cottons, the tight skirts and high heels contradicted by baggy, square-shouldered jackets and loose sweat-shirts. Women dressed for work.

Only when you look closely do you see that one is much older than the other, the tanned skin leathery, they're not really clones.

'I just didn't feel there was any communication any more –'

The younger one looks so sympathetic, she's buttering her colleague up, there's something in the air, a share in the boutique, maybe.

'And I just cannot seem to get him to see sense about the house. I mean it was my money that paid for it all, the carpets, the lounge suite, the aquarium –'

'He's not taking the aquarium!'

But the older woman is tired of her own troubles: 'So tell me about your sister and this Pakistani – how's your mother reacted?'

30

'Oh, she didn't really like it – no ... mind you, he's quite nice, quite attractive in his own way, but my sister's not like me, I mean I'm a strong person, I know what I want, but my sister, well, she's never really been in love before, she looks up to him *too* much, you know what I mean. She's given up the hairdressing, to help him. He's got quite a good little business, he makes these samosas in a garage he's rented in Saltdean, packs them up and sells them to the cafés, there's a tremendous demand, apparently, they're rushed off their feet, he needs a proper assistant, my sister's exhausted –'

Making samosas in a garage in Saltdean about sums up a whole level of entrepreneurship along the coast where so many – visitors and residents – are neither rich nor poor, neither professionals nor workers, the bricolage of the class system. Nouvelle cuisine and rag-rolled walls have been assimilated along with home computers. Downwardly mobile style; you know it's too late to have your walls professionally stippled when you realize that the Ramada Renaissance Hotel on Brighton sea front has chosen it for their entrance hall, which, with its floral-upholstered cane seating, looks like one of those up-market Indian restaurants that aim to evoke the Raj, but despite the sepia photographs and the chintz they never manage the one essential ingredient: shabbiness, which in those circles (I remember my grandmother's house again) was *de rigueur*. Nothing must ever be new. You had to have it for three generations before it was truly yours.

No one's even heard of the patina of generations down here. The man who came to lay the carpet moved from Croydon three years ago.

'I mean, you know why I got out –' pregnant pause – ' 'cos of the coloureds. You have to admit – it's true, what they say. I mean, I *know*. My son's friend got knifed in the stomach. I saw it myself. And the muggings –'

'Well, that's funny, because I live in a very white area of London, but it has the highest crime rate in the country.'

'Oh yeah – well, they're not *all* like that, I agree ... but you have to admit. You have to admit, it's gone too far up there.'

Then Brighton must suit him, because it's a very white town. But he says, 'I'm thinking of moving to Spain. Make even more money out there.'

Indeed, bits of Brighton are not unlike the Costa del Sol. Along the beach, under the cliff, there's a group that gathers round a little café, always the same couples; gender is exaggerated, the men wear exiguous jockstraps that disappear in the folds of a jutting beer belly; the women wear high-heeled mules, long varnished nails and leopard-printed bikinis flushed with gold. But both sexes wear heavy gold jewellery and a brick-red tan (haven't they heard of skin cancer?), and sunglasses.

There's another dimension to the seaside, though, the time dimension. As you drive along the coast road, here is the thirties forever embalmed. You've done it at last, got back into the past. All those semi-detached houses; there's Tudor beam and pebble-dash, and houses reminiscent of an ocean-going liner, with porthole windows, rounded corners to walls washed white and flat roofs with railings like a promenade deck – even if the steel window frames have rusted and the concrete cracked and stained. And then there is the Ocean View Hotel, perched on the slope of the Downs, with the name in big letters, as if this were Hollywood. Just the place to stop off for cocktails. Really so *wonderfully* thirties – and still in use as an hotel!

We tried it once. Passed through the Art Deco doors and found ourselves in a large, quiet crowd, immobile, penned in. We tried to move towards a door which said BAR, but it was locked, and beyond it we glimpsed a dining-room with the first course of a meal laid out; serried rows of orange soup and plates of bread and butter. Like an old-fashioned children's home. We looked round again – and *of course*: these little men and women, mostly women, were not children; they were the old. The place was being used as a holiday home for OAPs, bundled off here by the Social Services, and now they stood bewildered or cantankerous or passively grumbling as they waited for the dining-room to be unlocked. Not so different from the children's home, only at the opposite end of the cycle, old age herded together in a dystopia of functionlessness, rationed enjoyment for shrivelled beings who, in the mass, seemed not quite human. We drove away at speed, feeling young yet menaced, guilty too, the drive through the time-warp suburb ending in a glimpse of our own unwanted future.

People come here to die, to escape, to live out their fantasies. That's the Graham Greene side of Brighton, the seedy, tatty side of the big Edwardian houses in the hinterland behind the Front, where murders are committed behind dirty lace curtains, a stifling 1930s world. Many of the houses have been converted into up-market flats, and these days, even if there are still some rooms let by land-ladies interested in spiritualism and aspidistras, it's to the students with their punk hairdos and flapping black clothes rather than to frustrated clerks or retired governesses.

Last year, two little girls from a rundown council estate were assaulted and murdered in a local park. That's a more modern kind of murder than the between-the-wars kind, which was all mixed up with hopeless adulteries or the swindling of older, richer women by confidence tricksters who went too far.

The between-the-wars world lingers on, though: the palmists and the Tarot card readers on the pier and in the Amusement Arcade, and in the hinterland you glimpse worlds in which the search for identity and meaning takes particular local forms. Miriam and Christine, for example. In their North London days they dressed very sharp, very punk. Miriam was a radical Catholic then, involved in the Anglo-American lesbian feminist current within the Church. These days they're both more interested in 'the old religion'. They go to occult parties and have abandoned punk in favour of a slightly archaic mode of dress. Miriam has grown her hair and fastens a rose into its coils, and her long dress is decorated with macramé; Christine wears a brocade smoking-jacket with velvet trousers and embroidered bedroom slippers.

The political activism of the 1970s dissolves so that we more clearly see the links between now, the late 1980s, and the 1960s. Hippie mysticism persists. Rebellion takes the form of experimental art again, as demonstrations fade into the past. Conventional politics is now the outmoded and banal.

A young woman and man call to ask me a few questions about my religious beliefs, bombard me with multiple choice questions:

'Was Jesus Christ: (a) the Son of God; (b) a very holy man; (c) part of ancient myth and legend; (d) never existed.'

'The present state of the world is caused by: (a) the sin and wrongdoing of mankind; (b) evil rulers and world leaders; (c) is the work of the devil; (d) is not caused by anything.'

In attempting to explain the philosophical and logical problems these questions caused me I let slip that I'm an atheist.

'I know that's old-fashioned these days.'

'Mmm, that's interesting; that's *very* interesting,' says the young man. (The young woman with very long blonde hair and a very short denim skirt, says nothing.) 'Yes, you're right, *very* few people these days would call themselves atheists. We haven't come across many at all. Very few. Marxist . . . mmm, possibly, but there again, not many people call themselves Marxists either. *I* used to think of myself as a Marxist – I see myself more as a kind of anarchist Baptist now.'

Bricolage, recycling of the mind then, as well as of the broken coffee grinders and crimplene suits in Oxfam; there's the junk shop of ideas and theories, the second-hand bookshops, the stacks of old records.

Even Gay Brighton has changed, is more subdued. A friend described his first visit to the town, in the early sixties. For the first time he visited a gay club, and was enchanted by its red Regency flock wallpaper and candelabra wall lights, enchanted too by being taken to visit a famous literary queen who wrote columns for the women's magazines and gave lectures to the coffee-morning circuit about his garden. The camp humour quite bowled my friend over.

By the 1970s gays were very out in Brighton. But where are they today? I spotted a lesbian couple at the Theatre

Royal – a lot of *maquillage*, designer clothes, brilliant haircuts, the faint suggestion of butch and femme discreet to the point of disappearance. The gays seem privatized, apolitical, invisible. They lunch off croissant sandwiches and Perrier in the Sombrero coffee bar. Couples or not? Hard to know.

'I think you frightened him off at the very last moment,' said one. 'You tended to pounce a bit –'

'Yes. I got over-confident –'

'You have to remember there's a *very thin line* between making a sale and not making a sale ... but you know,' and here the voice of this, the more dominant of the two, or so it appeared, took on an exalted, even awed tone, 'sometimes I think we might be on the edge of making a *lot* of money ... and then sometimes I think we're not –'

New forms of tourism have developed in Britain. The Theme Park is the path to the future, according to a recent newspaper article: Wigan Pier has been turned into an Orwell memorial and history of the Depression in the North of England. Other places, the writer suggested, should follow suit, if they have not done so already. The traditional seaside resorts, however – the main subject of the piece – have failed to update themselves and have therefore not been able to cash in on the tourist boom. More persons than ever before, both British and from abroad, are taking holidays in this country, but they are not visiting the seaside, where profits have collapsed. A photograph of Brighton's crumbling West Pier illustrated the article: the only grade one listed pier in the British Isles and a paradigm of the fate that has befallen the lights, the amusement arcades, the dirty postcards and raucous promenades, the shivery beaches and bracing waves of our coastal resorts: the seaside resort of the industrial working classes. But it's hard to see how Brighton or Blackpool or Skegness could turn themselves into theme parks – a museum of tourism the size of an actual town. After all, unlike Wigan or Liverpool, Blackpool and Brighton have not been 'de-industrialized'. With all the talk of holidays abroad, the English seaside is still being used for what it was

35

originally intended: seaside holidays. (A recent Scottish bus strike during Glasgow Fair week, when by tradition Glasgow takes its annual holiday, caused chaos by preventing thousands of Glaswegians from taking the buses they had booked to Blackpool.)

And anyway, in Brighton at least there are the conferences, the arts and film festivals, the University. More important than anything, though, Brighton is for the flowering of eccentricity, and eccentricity is absolutely excluded from any theme park. A theme park is a postmodern invention, essentially a pastiche of the past rather than a memorial to it. Whatever its educational pretensions, a theme park is an expurgated edition, is more like Fisherman's Wharf in San Francisco, or Covent Garden; or York city centre, which pedestrian precincts and Laura Ashley and Crabtree and Evelyn shoppes have transformed into a musical comedy, Merrie England stage set, recalling a time and place that never was in the interests of overblown consumerism. A theme park is, in fact, not a museum – in which eccentricity might be to some extent preserved – but is a simulacrum. As a theme park Brighton as a living place would cease to exist. Its truth is too peculiar to be fixed or characterized. That is why it has the Pavilion, a bricolage of styles, a utopian fantasy, an exemption from rules and the historical evolution of architecture: a folly.

To be a theme park is to be dead. Brighton is alive; a cultural sponge that soaks up the contemporary experience and reproduces it in an intensified form. Fads and fashions are born here, out of the refuse of the intimate domestic world as cast on the junk heap of Oxfam. Everything is ephemeral, and the ephemeral can't be pinned down and municipalized.

Everything is ephemeral, that is, except the sea. You can stand on the shingle – in the winter is best – and watch the waves as they gather their watery muscle into a translucent knot, rear up, roll down and fan out in a foamy hem that disavows its power. It is so soothing to listen to the breakers sucking at the shingle, with a growl and a sigh, sliding shingle and the Aaah of the sea, a symbiotic embrace, the shingle forever rocked to and fro, milled together and ground, in another million years or so, to sand. You can often find a piece of broken glass that has been honed into a rounded pebble by the motion of the waves. On the edge of the sea nothing changes, there is only the water rushing at the shingle and falling back. And you could listen to it for all eternity, a sound that could even reconcile you to death.

7

Living Dolls

The first time I saw one was on the forecourt of the Beaubourg in Paris on a cold January afternoon. The cobbled square slopes upwards and away from the massed pipes, tubes and escalators of the art centre that towers above it; and 'he' was standing near the top of the slope. Onlookers had gathered, and we joined them. Our breath steamed into the dim grey air. The cold gripped us, slowed us down, it was painful to stand still.

He, though – but partly for this reason we murmured: it must be a – a what? – a doll, a statue, a clockwork figure – he did not breathe. No cloud of frozen breath escaped his lips. Nor did he shiver in his thin suit, while our hands and feet ached with it, and we huddled in our thick furs. The figure of a men's outfitters' dummy from the 1950s: hair slicked back, short back-and-sides; tan, clean-cut face, smooth as plaster; he wore a cheap fifties suit, white shirt, dark tie, lace-up shoes, and carried a small attaché case. He stood – had been placed – near a bollard: a piece of kitsch sculpture.

Suddenly his arm jerked upwards, he executed a half turn, brought his attaché case to a horizonal position, supported it with his other hand, snapped open the locks. The effect was uncanny – we watched compulsively with a mixture of euphoria that the imitation of lifeless lifelikeness could be so perfect, and disappointment that the moving statue was not a living doll but only a performer. In spite of the cold we found it impossible to tear ourselves away and we watched the dummy display the contents of his briefcase (a notebook, some sandwiches), walk a few

38

steps down the slope, pause, take up his petrified position again, then waltz into a new series of clockwork movements. At length a sense of the endlessness of the sequence, and our disappointment in deciding that the 'doll' was alive won out over our glee at the 'lifelike' imitation of unnaturalness, and we wandered down towards the art centre, casting backward glances at the waxen figure – who was still turning and stopping – somehow unsatisfied yet still thrilled by this inexplicable performance.

It is two-and-a-half years later; the tourist season in Florence. I've found a café near our hotel where they sell genuine 1950s postcards *as though they were new*. There is one of the Piazzale Michelangelo in which girls in circular skirts stand posed like something out of *L'année Dernière á Marienbad* – stuck in time past like the apparition at the Beaubourg.

In the evenings the Piazza della Signoria is crowded with American teenagers, with hippies, with a youthful international soldiery of pleasure seekers. There are entertainments: guitarists who sing the songs of the sixties – 'Blowin' in the Wind' and 'The Yellow Submarine'. There are fire-eaters, sword-swallowers and jugglers, just like the forecourt of the Beaubourg. In a side alley an especially large crowd encircles two performers . . .

A woman dressed as a man stands behind a hurdy-gurdy. S/he wears a waistcoat, rolled up shirtsleeves, dark striped trousers, a hat pushed to the back of her head, and a bow-tie: a figure from the slums of the twenties, Chicago, Naples, Petticoat Lane, anywhere, an old-fashioned organ-grinder.

Instead of a monkey, however, a giant doll flops at the feet of the organ-grinder, placed leaning against the machine. He stands her upright, balances her on her feet, sets her head and arms in place, then winds her up. Then he turns the organ handle and the plaintive music begins. The big-boned doll dressed in her plaits and apron and ballet shoes slowly turns, her arms move up and down, her head jerks left and right.

The mechanical dance ended, the organ-grinder ceases to crank out the tune from his organ, and sits his doll down again, her arms now holding her apron wide; and waits. There is a silence. Then, gradually, reluctantly, the crowd begins to drop coins and notes into her apron. The organ grinder stands impassive, leaning against his machine, he puffs a cigarette and watches, waits, and the doll sits rigid, smiling, open-armed. In the silence the coins, the notes are thrown towards the apron. But grudgingly – the crowd is waiting for something. A man leans down flaunting a large note, holding it just out of reach of the doll – nearer, pulled away, nearer again.

Dead silence. It's getting tense.

She cracks, and snatches it, laughing, but defeated. The spell is broken. The crowd, disappointed, moves away. The man has spoilt it. And yet they're pleased too.

We leave as well, not wanting to see the organ grinder and his doll depart. That would spoil it even more, seeing them 'behind the scenes', just two performers.

But I wonder about them. Do they travel through Italy performing their act – travelling entertainers as though it were still the nineteenth century? Are they lovers? Does the organ-grinder always treat her like a doll? Is it sado-masochistic? Does she always dress in men's clothes?

Now I'm hurrying through an intersection of the London underground system at Bond Street in the West End. At the bottom of a short escalator a brightly-lit esplanade opens out, and short passageways lead out of it to the platforms on either side. At the foot of one escalator a life-size Action Man twists and jerks. Combat jacket and camouflage trousers tucked into boots, leather gloves, a balaclava helmet – the outfit's complete; and this time the face is a plastic mask, so you can't know if there's a real person behind it or not. He's positioned himself so that the crowds emerging from the platform on his left confront him suddenly and unexpectedly as they turn towards the 'up' escalator. From the mouth of the opposite platform passengers waiting for their train watch, mesmerized. Some remain even when their train does roar down the tracks to a halt, riveted by the effect the twitching, epileptic Action Man has on the unsuspecting departing passengers who turn the corner and almost bump into him.

You're dying to stay and watch, yet vaguely feel you shouldn't. There's again the sense of shock, of mild horror. Yet you want it to go on forever. And at the same time there's a weariness as you watch because you also know that nothing is going to come of it, there's no conclusion, just the ritualized repetition of gestures, fetishized, a sort of artistic repetition compulsion.

What is this performance art that has sprung up spontaneously in late twentieth-century cities? It has all the postmodern fascination with surfaces, with play, with kitsch. The living human being alienates herself, himself, recreated as a thing, a doll. But is it simple alienation when individuals make of themselves objects that are works of pop art? They appear to comment on commodization, or on the dehumanization of the individual, yet at the same time to glory in it.

The art – the perfect imitation of a mechanized object, necessitating absolutely perfect control over one's body – is itself worthy of admiration, and a sort of test of endurance *('il faut souffrir pour être belle'),* but it is in the reactions of the audience that we must seek for further meanings of these street happenings. There is not the same unmixed pleasure as that with which we greet the skill of the dancer or musician or perhaps the acrobat, not even the cynical respect with which we watch the *trompe l'oeil* of the conjurer or the fire-eater, when we know a deceit is being perpetrated but still enjoy the skill whereby we are deceived.

There is something definitely unpleasant as well as terribly magical about these living dolls. Uncanny. The impossible idea of human beings turned to dolls is a theme of horror literature. There is also the theme of dolls that come alive in order to kill human beings, whereas the living beings who are turned into dolls suffer a kind of petrification or living death. So it is understandable if we feel relief when the masquerade breaks down and the doll is unmasked as a living person. What is less easy to understand is the unpleasure of this dénouement, the realization that we wanted the illusion to continue, wanted the person to be, really, a doll – wanted the magical, not the 'real'. This is not because we want the living person to be dead, but on the contrary because we want the doll to come alive – a common enough childhood fantasy, in any case, as Freud pointed out. Perhaps, therefore, our engagement in these performances is little more than the simple desire for the triumph of pleasure principle over reality principle.

The whole event remains, none the less, tinged with the uncanny, for behind the reassurance that all is well, that the doll *is* alive, is the opposite: a doll is actually not alive. Entwined in the tales of living dolls and humans turned to statues is the fear not only of castration, which is how Freud explained it, but of death itself.

In his discussion of the uncanny, Freud[1] associated some of these themes to the compulsion to repeat – the persistent re-enactment of past unresolved conflicts in the present. Perhaps this goes some way towards explaining our ambiguous reaction to these half-mysterious street performances. The fascination of the repeated movements, of the cyclical nature of the act – the pause, then the series of movements, then the caesura – reflects both the satisfaction and the unsatisfaction of the compulsion to repeat; which never succeeds in resolving the conflict buried in the past, because the conflict is simply repeated in a disguised form. The repressed only returns; is never transcended. But what collective repressed do these performances seek to exorcise? Each one is a tic on the face of the city, an aestheticization of malaise, saying something, we are not sure what.

So eventually the crowd turns away, sated but not satisfied, frustrated, cheated, yet longing for more, searching through the interstices of the city or the underground alleys of the modern labyrinth, the subway systems of the world, or in the public squares, gardens and piazzas, the city spaces created for leisure, searching for the magical figure, the fairy tale come true: who reassures us that we are, after all, alive, but also that we do not need to feel, that we too can become living dolls. With their desperate semaphore of gestures they mutely sign anxieties we can't even put a name to, in spaces of anomie where shopping is disguised as recreation – Covent Garden Piazza, or Fisherman's Wharf: unplaces for these unbeings. And it's unclear, 'undecideable', as they say, whether to transform yourself into a work of art is the supreme alienation or the supreme transcendence.

An essentially urban phenomenon: these performances can only achieve their effect in the anonymity of the crowd. The performance is instant; the living doll appears as if by magic, and at the end must disappear as quickly. Essentially urban because it replicates the experience of the crowd. The being, the living doll has banished all fear by being neither dead nor alive. Thus it is safe from the dangers of the city and symbolizes the feeling so typical of great city life: the feeling of semi-euphoria, of slightly dream-like disassociation. The living doll is like Edgar Allen Poe's 'Man of the Crowd', a restless wanderer, seeking to exorcise some guilt, seeking to escape, yet finding his being only in the crowd. These living dolls, too, live only in the crowd, it is the gaze of the crowd that gives them their 'life', they must have an audience, they have to be seen in order to exist. The private, for them, would mean extinction, so they must endlessly expose themselves to the ambivalent sadism, the gleeful indifference of the crowd, forever repeating the exaltation of a secular martyrdom, an aesthetic consummation that is forever only foreplay.

8

Chic Thrills

The industrial city: in its vortex all is changed, made strange. The anonymous urban crowds hide yet reveal all the new identities that individuals invent for themselves in this amazing environment where secrets are displayed yet masks worn, where you brush with suggestive intimacy against strangers in corridor-like streets, yet where neighbours and colleagues know nothing of your private life. Private life – street life: a gap widens between inner self and public presentation, and this makes new demands of dress. Fashion descends from the aristocratic courts of the *ancien régime* to beautify the lives of the urban masses. Daily life is aestheticized; soon mass-produced finery makes available a means of self-expression and self-display undreamt of in former times.

In the nineteenth century fashions ceased to originate exclusively with the upper classes. The bourgeoisie was in the ascendancy. Yet however much the bourgeois family might consume, however much the bourgeois home might be the theatre for extravagant display, and however much the bourgeois wife and daughter might aim to follow the latest fashion (or, according to Thorstein Veblen,[1] be destined to display the bourgeois male's wealth and prestige) they were inhibited from being fashion innovators by the very characteristics of bourgeois life that encouraged display: the conformity and anxious refinement of the bourgeoisie and its obsession with correctitude checked the spirit of competititon and emulation. Outrage had to come from elsewhere.

44

The fact that the *demi monde* is so frequently a pioneer in matters of fashion is due to its peculiarly uprooted form of life. The Pariah existence to which society condemns the *demi monde* produces an open or latent hatred against everything that has the sanction of law, of every permanent institution, a hatred that finds its relatively most innocent and aesthetic striving for ever new forms of appearance. In this continual striving ... there lurks an aesthetic expression of the desire for destruction.[2]

The *demi-monde*, by contrast with the bourgeois class, was well placed to innovate. Its men were the rebels, the artists, the dandies; its women had placed themselves outside polite society. The *demi-monde*, which included the artistic bohemia of the nineteenth-century cities, produced *arrivistes*, but could also include *déclassé* aristocrats as well as rebels from within the bourgeoisie itself. Whereas under the old order the bourgeoisie had represented the rising class in rebellion against aristocratic privilege, now it was against the established bourgeois order that the bohemian *demi-monde* rebelled, and, characteristically, its revolt took a cultural rather than a directly political form. At a time when the working class was repeatedly engaged in direct political struggle with the capitalists, there was also this double cultural division within the ranks, an intellectual dissent within the bourgeoisie, which expressed itself in an aesthetic rather than a political form; it was also transgressive, controversial, within the radical movement: 'dissidence' – a critique of what was rather than an aspiration towards what might be.

The dandies of the early nineteenth century developed a form of dress that expressed both the revolt of the bourgeoisie against the old upper-class order, and the subsequent alienation of the intellectual within the bourgeoisie: restrained, aloof, romantic. The province of women was in the realm of moral rather than intellectual dissent. By the exaggerated styles and extreme luxury of their attire the nineteenth-century courtesans defied polite society, and to the extent that they ruined the rich men who paid for their clothes and jewellery, they subverted the values of capitalist society in enacting the antithesis of

45

thrift, sobriety and accumulation. Or perhaps they merely displayed the other side of that society, its consumerism, in a gendered spectacle of contradictory antinomies symbolized in dress. Indeed, a marked feature of nineteenth-century dress was its increased differentiation of gender. In particular, male dress now became more heavily 'masculine', more stable, more to be contrasted with the frailty, frivolity and fickleness of changing feminine fashions. Women's dress might continue to play with some of the signs of male dress, but the reverse was less and less true. Effeminacy was ridiculed and feared – and gradually came to be associated exclusively with male homosexuality. (By contrast, the macaronis and fops of the eighteenth century, lampooned and ridiculed as they had been for their effeminacy, were associated not with sexual inversion, but with excessive heterosexuality and womanizing. They had been 'ladies' men'.)

Now it was the *demi-monde*, these male and female adventurers, individuals outside the family, who came from nowhere and had nothing to lose, who could afford to be most innovative in their personal appearance. Indeed, they had to be. For they aimed to succeed in a society that was no longer ruled rigidly by birth and breeding, by tradition and inheritance. Not that this society was not snobbish and status conscious; on the contrary, it may have been more preoccupied than ever with class, rank and breeding. But ultimately money ruled, and no one really knew where they were any more. It was the epoch of the 'self-made' man (or woman) – and in this world in which you could invent yourself, your appearance counted for more than ever before, and in a new way. Outsiders could 'pass' if they imposed themselves in a sufficiently convincing fashion. For them, daring in dress might be one way of making a mark on this society of appearances. Whether or not their dress, as Georg Simmel argues, expressed their underlying hatred of and contempt for polite society, it could be their passport to success.

Male homosexuals might well constitute part of the *demi-monde* in the exploding urban world. The industrial metropolis offered an anonymous environment freed from the constraints of family, in which the homosexual identity was able fully to emerge; but, precisely because of the anonymity of the city, the homosexual needed to be able to recognize those with tastes similar of his own. There therefore developed not only cafés and other haunts where the like-minded, by tacit consent, congregated, but also subtle dress-code indicators whereby homosexuals could recognize other members of the 'fraternity':

In their neighbourhood, where for the rest they mix only with brother students, teachers or some fellow-provincial who . . . can help them on, they have speedily discovered other young men who are drawn to them by the same special inclination . . . Applying to the object of their distraction the same utilitarian instinct, the same professional spirit which guides them in their career, they meet these young men at gatherings to which no outsider is admitted any more than to those that bring together collectors of old snuff-boxes, Japanese prints or rare flowers and at which, what with the pleasure of gaining information, the practical value of making exchanges and the fear of competition, there prevail simultaneously, as in a stamp market, the close cooperation of specialists and the fierce rivalries of collectors. No one moreover in the café where they have their table knows what the gathering is, whether it is that of an angling club . . . or of an editorial staff, so correct is their attire, so cold and reserved their manner, so modestly do they refrain from any but the most covert glances at the young men of fashion . . . [But] on certain evenings, at another table, there are extremists who allow a bracelet to slip down from beneath a cuff, or sometimes a necklace to gleam in the gap of a collar . . .[3]

By the turn of the century lesbians as well as gay men sought to distinguish themselves by their manner of dress. Toulouse Lautrec, the painter of Parisian low life, portrays his lesbians in mannish suits, though wearing skirts. Full cross-dressing 'was restricted by an ordinance passed in 1800 and, at the turn of the century strictly enforced by Lépine, the Paris prefect of police'.[4] Certain upper-class women, however, such as Colette's lover the Marquise de Belbeuf, known as Missy, were able to evade or even flout the law. But on the other hand, the more masculine style of suit for streetwear became an accepted fashion for all women in the early years of the twentieth century and by the 1920s fashionable dress had been transformed and had become androgynous.

Shari Benstock sees cross-dressing in the 1920s as:

a public announcement of a commitment to lesbian relationships ... registered ... in a code that specifically denied an allegiance to womanhood. ... Cross dressing constituted a simultaneous denial of the feminine and a taunting of male authority.[5]

She explains it in terms of the social privilege of upper-class women, and is critical of its lack of feminist conscious-ness. This may well be true, yet misses the almost mys-terious relationship of appearance to sexuality. Radclyffe Hall devotes a passage in *The Well of Loneliness* to what is almost an initiation rite. Mary, who has come to live with Stephen, the 'male' heroine, inspects her new lover's wardrobe rather as though it contains the mystery of Stephen's sexual nature:

Mary opened the wardrobe, revealing a long, neat line of suits hanging from heavy mahogany shoulders – she examined each suit in turn with great interest. ... On the shelves there were orderly piles of shirts, crepe de Chine pyjamas ... and the heavy silk masculine underwear that for several years now had been worn by Stephen.

Stephen's apparel almost *is* her sexuality, and her sexual attraction is mediated through her masculine garb and accessories – which also denote a strong class loyalty. Stephen's whole appearance in fact is designed to render her the simulacrum of an upper-class English gentleman – but with a difference, for at the heart of this masculinity is the vulnerability of her gendered fault, her ambiguity:

Stephen was ... grooming her hair with a couple of brushes that had been dipped in water. The water had darkened her hair in patches, but had deepened the wide wave above her forehead. Seeing Mary in the glass she did not turn round, but just smiled for a moment at their two reflections. Mary sat down in an arm-chair and watched her, noticing the strong, thin line of her thighs;

noticing too the curve of her breasts – slight and compact, of a certain beauty. She had taken off her jacket and looked very tall in her soft silk shirt and her skirt of dark serge.[6]

The glance in the mirror, the double reflections, mark both sameness and difference, the whole passage creating both an Other and a narcissistic love ideal.

The novel describes the smart lesbian circles of 1920s Paris, in particular the salon of Valerie Seymour, modelled on the real-life lesbian Natalie Clifford Barney. She was by no means masculine:

Valerie . . . was not beautiful nor was she imposing, but her limbs were very perfectly proportioned, which gave her a fictitious look of tallness. She moved well, with the quiet and unconscious grace that sprang from those perfect proportions. Her face was humorous, placid and worldly; her eyes very kind, very blue, very lustrous. She was dressed all in white, and a large white fox skin was clasped round her slender and shapely shoulder. For the rest she had masses of thick fair hair, which was busily ridding itself of hairpins; one could see at a glance that it hated restraint.[7]

Natalie Clifford Barney's lover was the painter Romaine Brooks whose portraits included one of Radclyffe Hall's companion, Una, Lady Troubridge, in a dandified costume complete with monocle. Anthony Powell, the chronicler of British upper-class bohemian life between the wars, describes a similar personage:

'Poor old Hopkins,' Norah said . . . 'Such a pity she goes round looking and talking like the most boring kind of man. Her flat might be the bar in a golf club' . . .
However, things had been very different some years before. Then, Hopkins had thrilled Norah and Eleanor with her eyeglass and her dinner-jacket and her barrack-room phrases.[8]

But now it was the 1930s, and the two younger women were caught up in political activity, in organizing support for the Spanish government against Franco's fascist troops, so that the affectations of an earlier decade had come to seem frivolous or perhaps even slightly ridiculous.

The lesbian bar culture of the 1950s preserved the distinction between what was now called butch and femme, masculine and feminine, a difference of which dress was the symbolic representation: 'butches were known by their appearances, fems by their choices.'[9] The difference was that this group of women was predominantly working class. Yet although the class connotations of fifties butch modes might be in contrast to those of the dyke dandies of the 1920s, they were equally – more – boldly oppositional. The 1920s had at least been a period when artistic modernism flaunted itself as a direct challenge to bourgeois society, one that perhaps claimed to transcend the customary forms of political revolt; the 1950s was a period of cultural as well as political conformity.

But from 1956 on, there was a revitalization of cultural and directly political dissent, and by the mid-sixties there was a questioning of masculine and feminine stereotypes, not only in the counter-culture, where men flirted with feminization, but also in mainstream fashion where women became androgynous and unisex became a cliché. At the same time, among 'progressive' lesbians the butch-femme roles began to seem reactionary and oppressive. In the male gay community too there was a reaffirmation in the 1970s of masculinity. For gay liberation, theirs was to be an army of lovers. The message was that homosexuals were not necessarily effeminate at all; it was not that they belonged to a third sex who hopelessly loved 'real men'; they themselves were 'real men' – if such a category meant anything.

Lesbians who were influenced by feminism encountered confusion. There was always a hidden agenda on fashion in the women's movement, but it was never argued through; the issues were clouded. Since feminism was, if not against men, certainly against 'patriarchy' or male power, and since it aimed to celebrate womanliness, a masculine style of dress must be a *faux pas* for a lesbian feminist. Oh the other hand a wholeheartedly feminine manner of dressing must also be viewed askance, since feminism offered a critique of fashion, perceiving it as part of the ideology that kept women in their place and positioned them as sex objects and nothing more.

How then to dress? An American feminist has described the net result as a kind of diluted butch look, which did not distinguish strongly between lesbians and heterosexual women. This seems to have been particularly the case in the United States where feminist counter-cultural dressing relied on garments derived from sports and student life – joggers, shorts, back-packs, trainers. Although these were much worn in Europe as well, other traditions were drawn on; there, feminists in the early 1970s created an 'arty' style with long skirts, second-hand frocks, velvet trousers and handmade woollies that was almost a re-creation of the 'socialist gowns' and 'artistic dress' of the 1900s, a style heavily reliant on hippie modes; and in the second half of the 1970s punk style was influential. But even the extreme avant gardism of punk (which also penetrated mainstream fashion) could not, despite its cutting edge, speak for lesbianism.

The androgyny of 'movement women' symbolized the downplaying of differences and potential divisions in the interests of sisterhood, but in signalling to the world that they were not sexual objects, both lesbians and hetero-sexual women might also lose ways of using appearance as a form of self-assertion. It has even been suggested that the repudiation of self-display was a form of self-hatred rather than what it was supposed to be and maybe felt like at the time: a statement of political ideals.

Within the lesbian community there was a further problem. One study of such a community, in an American mid-western university town, describes the problem as a problem of identity:

Within a lesbian community, we find that individuals constantly have to deal with the mirror images they present to each other and with the difficulty of developing a sense of self-identity that is different from the common identity that their group encourages. In this type of group, members must repeatedly improvise solutions which structure their relationships with one another so that they can emerge from experiences of loss of sense

51

of self with an identity that is different from the identity of others who look very much like them.[10]

Butch-femme dress codes had created sexual differences within the lesbian world, however spurious these had been, and their loss meant confusion. Some lesbians came to feel that their sexuality was suppressed rather than affirmed both by the political and by the sartorial definitions of 'politically correct' lesbianism, hence the re-evaluation of butch and femme relationships in the early 1980s:

Butch-fem relationships as I experienced them were complex erotic and social statements, not phoney heterosexual replicas. They were filled with a deeply lesbian language of stance, dress, gesture, love, courage and autonomy.[11]

Counter-cultural modes commonly act as a critique of and opposition to the dominant ethos of the culture in which they appear. Beats, bike boys, mods, bohemians, all have taunted the conformity of the world which spawned them; all have been transgressive. Lesbian and male gay dress codes in particular have set themselves a difficult task: to rework gender definitions. At different periods these codes have oscillated between two approaches: at one time there has seemed to be a clear alignment with gender character-istics of the 'opposite sex'; at another it seems more impor-tant to identify as a member of one's own sex, to be a womanly woman or a manly man. For women, however, *either* solution may appear or be experienced as oppressive and constraining, yet the androgyny of the centre can end up seeming sexless and self-effacing. Some lesbians do manage to combine both, that is to present themselves as both womanly and masculine – creating a radical dissonant chic, the outrage of bringing clashing opposites together, a sometimes haunting beauty of masculine presence at the very heart of femininity. This is the charisma of a Marlene Dietrich in drag.

Mainstream fashion, at all levels, is also about charisma. Nor is it only counter-cultural styles that have questioned gender. High fashion often plays, at least, with styles that interrogate the seamlessness of femininity; both *haute couture* and popular fashion are strewn with masculine hats, frogging, jackets, boots, ties and of course trousers. There is in all women's fashion as well as in lesbian dress a stylistic engagement with the masculine, with all its connotations of power, to underscore rather than to efface women's sexuality; to create an ambivalence which acknowledges that self-presentation is about power, that it is about one's ability to impose oneself on one's social environment. The dress codes of the lesbian and gay community have grasped this nettle, whereas the 'alternative' modes of other periods or other forms of radicalism have often shunned it, such power seeming a thing to avoid – consciously at any rate – in the interests of personal relationships freed from the exercise of power ... if this were possible.

What is clear from an examination of forms of dress developed by lesbians and gays is that dress is a necessary component in the construction of gender. In their case it is conscious and wholly deliberate; which is not to say that the same imperatives do not operate among heterosexuals, albeit at times subliminally. The heterosexual masculinity of a man is in part created by the armour of three-piece suit, sharply creased shirt collar, cuff links, 'masculine' gestures. Our appearance *is* in fact an appearance, a finished, constructed project, a gendered shell. This may not be true of all cultures, but it is true of ours. What is therefore unsettling about the cross-dressing aspects of lesbian/gay dress codes is their ability to make clear this construction, to display gender as a masquerade.

The 'out' gay identity lies at the interface of the biological body and its cultural vestments. Here, if anywhere, clothes clearly 'make a statement'. Yet the statement itself is ambiguous. To announce yourself, whether subtly or boldly, as one who loves the same sex, is not necessarily to call into question your own gender identification, although that is how it is commonly perceived. It could hardly be otherwise, given that these are sexual identities, and that lesbian and gay male sexuality – in appearance if nothing else – oscillates between the magnetic poles of masculinity and femininity. Sexual preference and gender identity tend

53

to get collapsed together, and this is as true in feminist writing as in mainstream psychological, psychoanalytical and sociological works and research. Gayle Rubin[12] is one feminist who has questioned this, and suggested their radical separation. Dress codes have none the less relied on the conflation, since there has seemed to be no other way of symbolizing desire and identity than to deck it in gendered form.

Of course, in contemporary society 'gay liberation', the philosophy of those individuals who choose to announce themselves publicly as 'what they are', usually using dress as well as other indicators, has been about more than simply the 'right to be gay'; it has been a fundamental questioning of social norms and customs and about the 'right way' to live. It is not surprising that the theoretician of 'carceral society', Michel Foucault, was gay. The ideological imprisonment of the homosexual, straitjacketed in a dictionary of pathologizing definitions has – perhaps particularly in the 1950s, when Foucault came to maturity – seemed almost seamless; the resistant, transgressive gay identity is identity as critique rather than as alterative, out to mess up prevailing gender identities rather than to create new ones. Their message is really the same as Freud's – that identities, specifically gender identities, are made not born, that, as Marx also said, we are determined by our social circumstances, but may choose to live these circumstances in varying ways, thereby to some degree altering them. This message is a simple but unsettling one. Nearly two hundred years after the industrial revolution which brought in its wake this other revolution of ideas, Western society is still struggling painfully with these unwelcome responsibilities, and trying to send them back to God, Nature or some other first cause.

In dress and adornment we are able to take up these struggles in a playful way. Yet even there bloodshed may occur, in the passionate disputes between the fashionable and the puritanical, the lovers of uniform and the lovers of nature, any position taken up liable to become a moral or a political one. Oppositional dressing has caused riots

– and persecution. Governments have been known to outlaw certain forms of dress.

Yet it is not always clear what new, or counter-cultural forms of dress are saying. In the 1970s both lesbians and gay men in the counter-culture drew back from femininity in dress. Yet there had been a recognition that femininity for both might be the most subversive gender message of all: because of the devaluation of femininity and women in the parent culture, feminine men and women who chose female lovers were defying and challenging the masculine ideal, the domination of maleness: but did it by appearing, in a strange paradox, more male.

As we edge towards the 1990s all fashion, including high fashion, engages in self-parody, and certainly bears no relationship to an entirely mythical return of women to the home. Oppositional fashions become parodic too. In 1986 the lesbian 'event of the year' in London was a ball at which women appeared glammed up in dresses, make-up, high heels. As parody and pastiche increasingly invade our lives we are all freer to make of fashion what we will.

Yet it still seems as if heterosexuality sets the parameters of the terms in which lesbian and gay men may be defined or may define themselves. Necessarily, since a transgressive gesture must always start from the boundary that is to be crossed, and only an impossibly utopian style could suggest some wholly other way to be.

Whereas urban culture, of which gay culture is a part, is not utopian, but is about survival in the city, which created gays.

9

Ariadne's Afternoon

It began to snow as I reached the Museum of Modern Art. I'd loitered all morning along First Avenue. When the cold began to bite I found a café at the end of a block, and from behind the glass shield of its plate-glass window I watched the parade go by. I counted fifty furs in five minutes. If I'd ever watched from a café window in Knightsbridge I might have seen as many furs, but never furs like these. Fur coats along Knightsbridge would be just another British uniform: beige mink. Here, a fur, far from being a mark of class solidarity, was rampant individualism, the owner's bet on the poker hand of her life. There was every style from tailored sable trenchcoat to Afro coat of crinkly unborn lamb. Career women hunched by with ten thousand dollars' worth of snow leopard or long-haired monkey draped across their bony shoulders, while their faces flowered brightly above – bronze-striped cheekbones, eyes hollowed with African violet, lips like poppies. These women stalked their prey as if they meant it. Not for them a loiter round the Harrods food hall. Their high-heeled boots stamped the frozen pavements as they clenched briefcases and hailed taxis.

Their consorts – bankers, movie moguls? – wore fur coats too, strode along in beaver and raccoon en route for some new financial frontier, bears in a bull market. By comparison with their mates – lacking the mask of *maquillage* – they looked a little drawn around the mouth above the astrakhan lapels. The eyes behind the Madison Avenue glasses were anxious, even hunted, and although the thinning hair was cut to hang boyishly over the forehead, a

56

twitch in the smartly shaven cheek betrayed the strain of perpetual oscillation between gym and gourmet restaurant.

It was a middle-aged crowd, haggard with wealth, intent and weary. The faces were not so different from those you saw on the subway or on the Staten Island ferry – immigrant faces, staring blankly inwards at unfulfilled dreams. The difference was that up here in this part of town they had their dreams by the throat.

I walked to the centre of Manhattan to see the de Chirico exhibition. The stuff for sale in the shop, the t-shirts, the books, had the logo, MOMA. Infantilizing – 'Moma' was the sort of name a zoo would give a baby gorilla, rejected at birth by its mother, who was institutionalized, and publicly hand-reared behind glass with all the trappings of bottles, nappies and progressive wooden toys littering its cage, from which it stared out at the laughing crowd, its world-weary face framed in a frilly bonnet.

'Moma' was meant, I supposed, to domesticate the wild animal of modern art. For among the incomprehensible objects, the china urinal, the action painting (surely a gorilla could have thrown that paint at the canvas, Moma herself) someone had caught sight of a lurking monster, a Minotaur, a King Kong. 'Moma' was a placating gesture towards that monster, in the edifice that housed it.

In the exhibition a group of elderly Jewish women argued about Chirico with their lecturer-guide. Was he a fascist? A sequence of irrational landscapes was littered with symbols from the unconscious. An orange rubber glove hung down beside a Greek head. In each painting a semi-human figure – broken statue, dressmaker's dummy, unstrung puppet – passively centred itself, a blank ego in empty city squares, in piazzas and desert vistas dreaming in the midday sun.

A plump, dark young woman in a grey tracksuit stared at a painting entitled 'Ariadne's afternoon'. Her eyes were bright and opaque as boot buttons, her pallid face filmed with grease or sweat. She smiled insistently at the affectless landscape, then sidled up to a stocky young college boy and engaged him in conversation. Did he like it? Did he visit art exhibitions often? Did he have a girlfriend? Her voice – she'd been speaking rather loudly – dropped to a mumble. The young man's face went red and he moved quickly on to the next painting. But she followed him, still smiling, staring, murmuring. He moved on again, faster. She followed. I lost sight of them in the crowd.

One room of the gallery led into the next, it was like a dream – Chinese boxes, a maze in which the string of paintings led you further and further into the set of rooms that led one out of the other. Only this maze had no centre, no secret at its heart.

Half an hour later I caught up with her again. She had drawn close to another young man and pinioned him with her smile. This one got rid of her more brutally. "I'm not interested,' he said, quite loudly. But nothing shook the fixity of her smile. She began to stalk a third, a older man. We moved apart again. Later still I caught sight of her as she trotted through the exit turnstiles, still smiling, still alone. I thought how cold she'd be, dressed only in a tracksuit with, it looked like, nothing underneath, as the icy granules of snow floated down in the dusk. But perhaps the mad don't feel the cold. No fur coat for her, anyway.

'The store *is* overwhelming!' sympathized the floor-walker in Bloomingdales, her smile melting through a mask of make-up. Blasts of heat pumped through the harem, the hot flush of selling. The dazzling aisles led me onwards down vistas enlarged by reflections from walls of mirror glass. At every turning young women accosted me. Their smiles were as insistent as Ariadne's, and as unshakeable, as they sprayed scent over me, pressed trial-size pots of face cream into my hands, or scented hankies. One was dressed as the Spirit of Spring, another as a Japanese geisha, a third in Arabian Nights silks; and there was a new Jean Harlow make-up – the lipstick, called 'lava', was almost black – held out by a Jean Harlow look-alike in cream satin with cream-coloured platinum hair. The fancy dress spirits of commerce beckoned me further and further into the maze. At the heart of it somewhere Beauty lay sleeping, the New Self ready to be awakened by one's own, narcissistic, kiss of life.

The Beast waited too, outside somewhere in the stinging snow and the paint strokes of neon that bled into the darkness. Everywhere I went everyone talked of muggers, rapists, senseless murders. Each death revealed the Beast who was always there. At any moment the tired, greedy crowds might part and the Minotaur appear – stand there, rearing up, standing like a man, but with hooves and a head like a beast.

You could never forget the monster, not for long, as you prowled the canyons between the glass cliffs and the towers of embroidered stone.

Up on Morningside Heights, near Columbia – 'Columbia': the ghost of a whole continent, central America, the silences of the Amazon, the sixteenth-century explorers, awed, terrified, silenced by the immensity of the jungle, a vast, vegetative cathedral, an inhuman, waiting labyrinth. The Avenue of the Americas must surely lead straight to the heart of that darkness, to Columbia, to the Amazon, to the Chirico city squares of Lima, Peru.

I could not sleep. Some nights the phone rang, late, later, after two a.m. I stumbled out to answer it, but there was only ever a furred, clicking silence.

Someone walked up and down in the next room. I crept naked through the shadows. The thief, restless with guilt, paced up and down. The room was empty, but the intruder walked to and fro, I could hear him. I stabbed my foot on an earring, cried out with pain, reached for the light, and the dusty little room stared back at me. I wrapped myself in a robe and huddled in a chair, switched on the television. Black and white images: an obese plainclothes cop watched a New York waitress through the plate-glass window of her restaurant, sloped after her through the mist and rain of a dank, wintry evening.

There was a tap-tap against the window. I pulled aside the curtain: a loose cable swinging in the wind.

The central heating system creaked and groaned into action, knocking and banging. The rooms grew hotter and hotter. I looked in the fridge for some alcohol to knock me

59

out, took a couple of pills, swallowed in gin, lay down in the dark. Couldn't sleep.

Light began to leak through the blind. I buried my face in the pillow, dozed for a moment, was jerked awake again by the white glare.

Christ, it's ten o'clock.

I'd arrived in an unexpected blizzard. Now a heatwave was welling up from Harlem. From the heights of embattled, fortified Columbia I looked down at the burnt-out buildings and empty streets of Harlem. Far over to the right the silver propelling pencil of the Chrysler building pointed skywards through the sooty haze. A boudoir murmur melted out over the airwaves: 'It's twenty-two degrees Celsius in mid-town Manhattan; have a very pleasant day.'

I climbed down through the little park. Flights of grey stone steps descended past stone urns and leafless grey creepers. Grey lichen clung to the balustrade. It was deserted. I turned a corner.

There stood Ariadne. Still in her grey tracksuit she stood talking to a man. They moved off together towards a dark mouth – a tunnel, or cave, fringed with the frothy curls of old man's beard.

At the bottom of the park the wide streets were deserted. The big red houses had been gutted, were all boarded up. This was a ghost town. I wandered deeper in, there were not even any shops, just some kids shooting up under the tracks of the elevated. Just silence; empty vistas.

Clutching a brief-case he hurried towards me out of the emptiness.

'Gee – I obviously got off at the wrong subway stop – there must be another 116th Street – can you tell me, is Columbia *any*where near here?'

I gestured back towards the little park.

'Is it *safe*?'

'I'll walk back up with you.'

'My, but it's eerie.'

We passed a man on the stone stairs in the little park. I wasn't sure if he was the man I'd seen with Ariadne. No sign of her now, the tracksuit woman. But the man . . . he was alone now, anyhow. Ariadne was gone.

I strolled down Broadway with the Upper West Side crowd, jostling for space with the students, the bohemians, the wealthy. A black Adonis dressed in white cut through on roller skates, flying ahead of us all. The crowds along the pavements were buying – asparagus and spinach, red and green peppers, grapefruit and pineapples, they sat in the café windows to eat ice-cream and croissant sandwiches, and loitered to read the books on the stalls in front of the shops, and flip the racks of summer clothes.

Among them shambled the men and women with paper bags, or sat on the sidelines. In the winter they lived in the subway. Now they were coming out of hibernation, disgorged onto the streets from emptied mental hospitals. Each had a pitch, a style, a patter, buskers whose acts had come unhinged. In the city of commodities they called their wares but found no buyers.

This city was amazing. Men and women hunted through the labyrinth for the secret heart of pleasure. From one interlocking room to the next they hurried on, as obsessed as the mad in their search. Ariadne roamed the geometric city.

In a bookshop I looked up the legend of Ariadne. Ariadne was the princess who gave her lover a thread that would lead him out of the labyrinth after he'd reached the centre and killed the Minotaur. Only the legend had changed in Manhattan. Here it was Ariadne who braved the labyrinth. And who is to give her the lifeline back to safety, from the heart of the maze.

10

The Counterfeit Detective

'In their works, part of the bourgeois pandemonium is exhibited.'

Walter Benjamin

They say that in a dusty back room of some London postal sorting office, there sits a functionary whose sole task is to open and answer the sackfuls of letters that are still arriving every day for Sherlock Holmes at his 221b Baker Street address. This bureaucrat is directed to send a standard answer which regretfully informs each inquirer that Sherlock Holmes has retired to the country.

The anonymous recipient of these last ditch appeals is a kind of agony aunt of the public sphere. The real agony columns of the women's magazines and the tabloids deal with problems of the private sphere: an unfaithful husband, the inability to attract a boyfriend, a difficult daughter, or how to cure acne – these are the moral and hygienic dilemmas of the family, the body and the home. The letters addressed to Sherlock Holmes seek solutions to these problems at a later and more developed stage, when they have invaded the public world. The conflict between parents and teenage children has become the drama of flight and disappearance, and the adolescent tyrant has become the victim adrift in the great city of pleasure and danger. The faithless lover has become an absconding confidence trickster, the man who extracted an older woman's money with a smile and a kiss, or the adventuress who destroyed a man's life for his wealth.

The letters to Sherlock Holmes do more than seek advice; they demand satisfaction, a solution, the end of the story. There is nothing so terrible as an unfinished story. There *must* be an unravelling to the story, we *must* know the truth, the whole truth and nothing but the truth. The mystery must be unravelled, like the thread that led Theseus away from the minotaur, out of the labyrinth. But this unravelling must lead the counterfeit detective *into* the contemporary labyrinth: the city that must be the setting for all such journeys of discovery. Sherlock Holmes and his latter-day deputy can exist only in the bureaucratized setting of modern urban life. In the vastness of the city it is so easy to be lost, and so difficult to find the truth. The mystery assumes the mournful anonymity of the great cities, of individuals adrift with no ties of kin, or friendship, or love on which to depend.

It is all different in the country house or village murder story, fables of enclosure in which the sleuth, Miss Marple or Adam Dalgleish, come from outside – and yet within – to assist in the restoration of rural or institutional normality, which seamlessly laps together again *afterwards*. They are of the same class as the members of the beleaguered world they exorcise. In the city version, the encounter between private eye and client, a meeting of strangers, is also between two members of the same class, the class of exiles from class, the lumpen bourgeoisie. Their meeting is mediated by the cash nexus (never the case with Miss Marple, whose perspicacity is an apotheosis of the spinster gossip and busybody, nor with Dalgleish and the other Good Policemen, who are part of the welfare state of law and order).

Sherlock Holmes has retired to the country to enact the role of gentleman. His counterfeit, however, sitting in a dusty room in the honeycomb of the bureaucracy, surrounded by the massed pigeon-holes and compartments of the sorting office, an official granted immunity by the state, positively enjoined to violate the privacy of the sealed envelope, to pry into the secrets of Sherlock Holmes's unknown correspondents, inevitably becomes more of a private eye, a Chandler hero, than a gentleman amateur.

I imagine how he (I say he, although gender is of only secondary importance in these cases: Miss Marple is a spinster, Dalgleish a widower, Philip Marlowe a bachelor with aggressively normal appetites but no time to satisfy them. What distinguishes them is celibacy, not gender), I imagine how this fake might have initially taken on the assignment as a joke. To begin with he laughs at the gullibility of those who write in from all over the world with naive trust in the ability of the great detective to solve their pathetic stories – often ill-spelt and ungrammatical – of missing relations, stolen legacies and threatened lives. To begin with he is content to respond with the standard answer.

'These crazy people.' It's a good story in the pub, anyway.

But gradually it becomes depressing, overwhelming. These fragments of other lives are grim and tantalizing, bits of flotsam cast up on a bleak beach. It develops into an obsession, a thirst to find out more, a compulsion to write back. These stories haunt his leisure hours, his private thoughts, most of all, his dreams.

Sooner or later there must come the letter that makes him crack. No longer can he resist the temptation to launch himself into engagement. He has a struggle with his conscience, agonizes over an act which seems as guilty as a crime, it's beyond his terms of reference, he was never told to do this. He was not told not to do it, for no one ever imagined that he would.

Had the stories been complete, he would have been content to remain a voyeur, a reader. It is the intense irritant of the repeated frustration of his fantasy that compels him at last to cross the shadowy border between imagination and enactment.

He writes back. This simple transgression involves deceit, or at least subterfuge, for now he must construct a persona for himself, find a place where they can meet. A café, the foyer of a hotel, perhaps; particularly the hotel lobby, a counterfeit drawing-room for the un-family of the traveller.

In any thriller the first meeting of detective and client is fraught with meaning while seeming opaque and trivial.

Like love. It is in the nature of these individuals who swim up to the surface in the first page or two that their mystery invests them with charisma, even though to begin with their satanic meaningfulness may be veiled. In this case – but it is always like this – the woman he meets (although it could be a man) is enigmatic from the start and if only for that very reason must be in some way beautiful. Personality wafts like a scent across the foyer, across the page. Whatever else, this person is *significant*. The sham detective, just like the real detective, lets himself slip under the spell. In doing so he takes the first step away from safety. He stands at the mouth of the labyrinth.

Of course, what she has come for seems innocent, unremarkable. She wants him to find her brother, say, to trace the family ne'er-do-well, something like that. Nothing complicated, although maybe a little sad. And as token of her trustworthiness she hands him, not money (although she *does* hand him money as well, but that's no guarantee of anything, despite being their only unambiguous link) but a clue. Again it could be anything – an address, a ticket, a pair of cuff-links.

From the beginning he knows, of course, the counterfeit detective knows he's playing a lonely game. He's stepped into the role of knight in armour, hero, he's laid claim to special virtue, special powers. He is the honest man who walks down the mean streets. He is *above* the sublimely monotonous world he inhabits, godlike in giving meaning to it, even if it is meaning of a strangely arid kind. Yet he is a fake. He is no knight in shining armour, but merely a bureaucratic mouse, originally chosen for his conformity, his routinized personality, his docility and lack of imagination. And now, moreover, he has become a fantasist, someone who in yielding to a compulsion has shown weakness rather than strength.

The course of the murder mystery proceeds in a ritualized way, like the stations of the cross. At each significant point a complication develops. The brother is found, but claims not to be the brother, or there is no brother at the address, or there is a brother, but he's been murdered. His death, disappearance or denial does not occur, however, without the dropping of another clue, by means of which reader and detective may be led further into the maze. But each clue the detective deciphers only at some personal risk, for the further in he goes the more dangerous it gets. And the more stations on the path he passes, the more he learns about the original client, the charismatic one, and thus the effect of the search is to unwind her from her web of mystery. His motive, even if unacknowledged, is his obsession with her, and he cannot allow himself to recognize that in solving the riddle she has set him he is destroying the very thing that fascinated him in the first place: her.

A cliché of romantic literature but a gripping one; and it has special resonance in the adventure of the detective. For his adventure is always a journey towards disappointment, banality, anti-climax. The ending of a thriller is always an ending of closure. It's like pornography: a compulsive search for relief, release, which returns the reader to the inertia of non-excitement.

The woman who initially appeared as a suppliant, as a fellow heroic seeker of the truth, or as a poignant victim, is progressively revealed as just another fake. She's playing a lonely game as well, and by the end she's bound to be in ruins. Despite appearances to the contrary, she is – well, she is only appearances. Her truth is to be eaten up by the past, and the deciphering of that past shatters the illusion of her mystery. Her mystery, her charisma is an illusion; she really isn't there at all.

Even the solution to the mystery still frustrates. It's less like a novel than like one of those case histories of Freud, which fragment as you read, in which there's never a future, only the iron grip of the past. And all these characters too are in the grip of a past without a future. Unlike ours, their story is finished, right from the start.

Having said that the sexuality of the detective is curiously downplayed (although never questioned), the romantic dénouement need not take a traditionally heterosexual form. It need not even be acknowledged as erotic desire at all, and, should it take a homosexual form, so much the better, so much the more impossible, more unspoken, more latent. Even if sexual desire should be openly played out, that is merely another mask, for one necessity within the detective story is the reassertion of the loneliness of the sleuth. Only his loneliness guarantees his immunity to the corruption all around him. The role of the detective is to be different from the others. He reminds us that there *is*, after all, normality, truth. Everyone else may be playing a double game; he, however, is not.

This detective, however – the counterfeit detective – is himself phoney. And a fake detective can hardly act as a stabilizing point; is bound, in the end to become part of the vortex of illusion. Instead of the destruction of ambiguity, ambiguities must multiply as the status and motives of the pretended Holmes become less and less clear.

A clerical assistant assigned to dispose of the results of a confusion in the minds of an anonymous public between reality and fiction, his own position is fictional, unstable and open to multiple interpretations.

Yet what does become clear, as he becomes more enmeshed in his enactment of illusions, is that the real detectives were equally false. The real detective is as anonymous as the clients, the victims and villains. The detached scientist, Sherlock Holmes, whose rational neutrality assures his dependability,[1] or the honest man in the mean streets – these are illusions too. In the urban setting there is *no* real centre of normality, and to that extent the honour of the sleuth is a sham. Both the real Sherlock Holmes (or Philip Marlowe) and the counterfeit detective live in a featureless flat in some region of drear urban monotony; both work in the anonymous interstices of office blocks, frequent bars, have few friends, no home life – it's a world of take-aways, streets, public places. The detective too is empty, the only difference from his heroine being that in the normal course of events his mask is never removed, no one ever unmasks him, since he is there to unmask the others.

This is one reason why the sleuth is celibate; it is part of the mask, part of *his* unknown-ness, part of his mystery, which, unlike that of the clients, the murderers and dead bodies with whom he deals, must never be dissolved. Sexual reticence, therefore, is appropriate to him. He too is outside the family.

For this reason, a recent sub-genre, gay liberationist or lesbian feminist crime fiction, fails to touch the exactly right chord: the engagement of the detective with an oppositional, or counter-cultural 'right side', an alternative good cause, destroys his omniscient and imperturbable overvision, that which, fraught with irony and indeed cynicism, hints at the world-weariness of which crime fiction is the expression; also, the investigator's allegiance to radical sexual politics implies an optimistic view of the world, a possibility of improvement, hope that right will triumph over wrong and in so doing cause a shift in the social paradigm; whereas the true world of the sleuth – notwithstanding his official role as the upholder of right and sanity in the world of mean streets – is actually a world without hope, and the 'right' (the normative order) the classic sleuth upholds is in no way radical, in no way implies social change; on the contrary it is the repressed that it is to return us to, the status quo ante, repression must be reimposed on the chaos that threatened to escape. He is in pursuit of the Other of his culture, the surface of which is represented as gloom, ennui, monotony:

Bunker Hill is old town, lost town, shabby town, crook town. ... In the tall rooms haggard landladies bicker with shifty tenants. On the wide cool front porches, reaching their cracked shoes into the sun and staring at nothing, sit the old men with faces like lost battles.

In and around the old houses there are flyblown restaurants and Italian fruit stands and cheap apartment houses and little candy stores. ... And there are ratty hotels where nobody except people named Smith and Jones sign the register ...

Out of the apartment houses come women who should be young but who have faces like stale beer ... worn intellectuals with cigarette coughs and no money in the bank ...[2]

but while this world is colourless and grey, the underworld it only just conceals is lurid with all the passion, intensity and exaggeration that must never be allowed to hold sway. A fascist narrative, therefore, rather than simply a conservative one, since fascism manages to celebrate the Id and the Superego simultaneously.

And the detective, armoured in irony, emotionally and sexually withholding, is the ultimate dandy, frozen in each successive moment of his being. For the dandy also seeks to arrest time, to restore a previous state of things, or a state of things that never was, when the self was perfect, cleanly delineated and defined with every gesture and every detail contributing towards the totality of a unified and perfect whole; the consummate *appearance*; appearance reified, appearance as a work of art. It is typically the dandy's role to reduce self to a solution in terms of presentation; it is the detective's role to reduce the flux of life to the dimensions of a perfect puzzle, that, when each piece has clicked into place reveals its own lifeless solution.

But, if the detective is a voyeur, the dandy is a blind observer, whose role in life is not to see but to be seen. He thereby dominates. He imposes his appearance on all others, who are compelled to imitate him. In a different way, but similarly, the detective imposes his solution on the others. He has got it right; they must accept his solution. And although the sleuth always claims to have arrived at the solution by force of logic, really he has imposed his solution by force of will. It is a triumph of the will. For the detective too is a faker, he goes down the mean streets just like anyone else, his superiority a sleight of hand, he has the luck of the gambler, another kind of dandy, not the brain of a genius, as Hercule Poirot would have us believe.

And the sleuth only poses as hero, for really the detective and the dandy are alike also in this, that (although many detectives both in life and in fiction are policemen and thus agents of the state) the archetypal detective is the marginal man, who, like Beau Brummel came from nowhere – no family, no lovers, no background, no calling, no money – and exists by virtue of his will alone.

11

Modern Heroes

The obvious, perhaps too obvious, candidate for contemporary hero is the young man in the money market, lighting the fireworks of the Big Bang (even after the Big Crash), eating treacle roly-poly in a City restaurant and driving home in his BMW or whatever will be the class car in 1990. Twenty years ago he would have been a pop star, a hairdresser or a photographer (as in Michaelangelo Antonioni's 1967 film, Blow Up); now he could be a young Tory, a narcotics dealer, an art dealer, an estate agent or an electronics engineer. He couldn't be any of the things that seemed groovy in the sixties, such as pop sociologist, television personality or clothes designer. But the obvious choice – the financial whizz kid – is as usual the most likely. (Let's pause to consider what the hero of the year 2010 will be: someone we won't find easy to predict, that's for sure.)

Today's hero must, if ugly, be sexy and sexually active as well, since everything must go against the grain, there must be a constant clash of dissonances, and the man must triumph by force of will; only if beautiful, therefore (a beauty achingly marred by a few pustules and wet-look hair gel still), may he be bored by sex or bad at it. He must be egocentric, but unselfconsciously so, and must spend his life surrounded by machines. He mustn't have anything as déjà vu as a suntan, a Filofax, a subscription to *The Face*.

His parents may be members of what used to be called the working class, or they may be middle-class health freaks who drink thin milk and jog round the Heath. It doesn't

70

matter what they are, because he has no time for Freud and introspection and absolutely no interest in the family romance. The past and childhood is a wipeout and on the one hand a working-class background (how *that* was prized in the sixties) is irrelevant; on the other he smokes, drinks and eats like there was no tomorrow. He does deals all week, work surfeit, overkill, and then it's overkill at weekends – two days in bed watching videos, doing some sport to death, compulsive socializing.

He is a far cry from the hero of *Blow Up,* which was a film by a very sixties director, the Italian Michaelangelo Antonioni, about a sixties hero. That hero was played by narcissistic, baby-faced cherub David Hemmings in self-congratulatory vein. Whether the narcissism was in the actor or in Antonioni's conception of the character we can't now know, but an even more intense narcissism would have to be the mask of the 1990 hero. In that respect the two are alike; what makes the David Hemmings character impossible for today is his flirtation with political commitment. We first see him emerging, disguised as a tramp, from a dosshouse, where he's spent the night gathering material for a photo realist dossier exposing the scandal of homelessness. And he's a searcher for the truth; the mainspring of the film's plot is his attempt to discover what happened when, as he believes, he accidentally photographed a murder in a deserted park.

He's rich(ish), but the things in life that only money can bring are attached to him casually, and his clothes and studio signal simplicity rather than opulence. Finally, he's an Artist, a witness, someone who lays claim to a privileged moral view of the world.

Today's hero has little interest in power. He's cynical about it. And he's certainly no Artist. Essentially he's purposeless, but money fills the vacuum. Money's the mainspring for today's hero. But it's not the things that money can buy that he values, although he's developed a dependency on his machines; and he might have one collector's obsession: say for Piranesi drawings or cigarette cards; or he might not care for cultural artifacts at all, might be into gambling or speedboats or holidays in South

East Asia, it could be anything, and it will have this irrational, isolated, fetish quality; but really he's just into money, and all these forms that it can take are less important than the thing itself, which is the element in which he lives, and each manifestation of it, from new car to espresso machine to multi-jet super-shower, is but an imperfect approximation to the idea of money itself, invisible as air. That is why the machines have to be continually discarded and replaced by newer models, with fewer defects, and which thus interfere less with the free-flowing *absence of discomfort* which is the essence of having money. No waiting for food or preparation of it; from freezer to microwave in five minutes; the kettle must boil instantly; the word-processor respond without delay. Thus does money annihilate everything, including the dimensions of space and time, rendering everying else to its own nullity.

So, if this contemporary hero is to be a tragic hero, what gets him will have to be fraud, or gambling, something money-related; or death by machine. Lust, for bodies or for power, would be too old-fashioned. Or maybe his tragic fault will be to have feelings. The contemporary mode has to be the deadpan amoral, feelings are a gaffe or a gas, as embarrassing as throwing up in public (although there are occasions on which it might be all right to do that). So maybe this man will die by a decent feeling.

Could he be black? That would be difficult, because that would bring in oppression, which is entirely out of place. It would be difficult for a black modern hero not to appear either too sympathetic or, if unsympathetic, then merely a racist stereotype. And we don't want any morality here. In any case British society is too racist for the creation of an ambiguous black character, rich as the lives of black citizens may be with bitter ironies.

Impossible for this hero to be a woman either, yet he must have as his female counterpart one who is more than a stereotypic cypher. This young woman – or there may be more than one – she, they, may have high tech jobs too, but they don't care so much for the technology in itself, or even perhaps for the money, he's not sure what they care about, they're all a little crazy, out of control underneath, they get too high and strip off at parties or lock themselves in the bathroom. Their mothers have sometimes got some creepy alternative religion, or they might train horses in the country. But equally these girls might be the daughters of policemen or teachers or electricians.

Gamini Salgado[1] likens the English revenge tragedies of the closing years of the reign of Queen Elizabeth I and the first decade of King James I's reign, the beginning of the seventeenth century, to the modern thriller. These popular Jacobean plays, he says, are a form of 'tragic satire', that is, while they adopt the satirical, scathing, moral approach to human folly, they point up not its richly comic but its tragic, nihilistic side; grim humour without humour, death without redemption, lust without either grace or absurdity.

The 'Italy' in which so many of these plays are set is, he argues, a moral dystopia in which poison is a kind of essence of 'Italian-ness' and murder is a short cut to success, a concomitant of intrigue. Secrecy is the counterpoint to appetite or desire; in a world in which politics are aristocratic the pursuit of individual obsession, ambition and lust necessarily takes a secret, private path.

Despite the religious gloss on sentiment and language, the world in which these saturnine men and women live is entirely secular, and therefore the Christianity in which they clothe their feelings rings hollow and merely adds a touch of cynicism. This is a world of unbelief, of negation.

Most modern thrillers are not quite tragic satire so defined (although the works of Jim Thompson certainly are). In the majority a conservative, conventional moral universe remains implicit. The contemporary detective may have lost some of Sherlock Holmes's Olympian authority, and may himself be puzzled or menaced by the events he undertakes to investigate, but the world in which he moves still operates according to the implicit moral values that to some extent we continue to take for granted, however inert these have become. The contemplation of evil takes on a patrician, conservative and melancholy cast with British detectives such as P. D. James's Inspector Dalgleish; or dashes against the incorruptible lone ranger or little man, which is what Philip Marlowe stands for: a world of pre-urban, simple values. Dalgleish is aloofly appalled by the depths to which human nature can sink if allowed to step outside certain socially sanctioned and enforced moral restraints. And very often, still, it is the old staples of sex and class that define the boundaries of good and evil. Today, as in the Agatha Christie period, villains are surprisingly often lower middle class, homosexual or foreigners. (This is also true of Paul Scott's novel sequence *The Jewel in the Crown,* although they are not, of course, thrillers.) Despite a recent vogue for countercultural thrillers, and the classic exception of Dashiell Hammett, most books in the genre are not exactly Left wing. And this should not surprise us, since the stability of the existing order necessarily underlies a struggle against 'evil' and 'destructive forces', and in a popular work must depend on popular cultural understanding of what stability and order imply. In spite, therefore, of the moral and political corruption that many thriller writers describe and openly acknowledge, their very condemnation, indeed the *raison d'être* of the thriller – the search for and destruction of the evil characters, organization or plot – gestures towards a moral order that is not thus overturned. To this extent the thriller differs from 'tragic satire'.

Yet how easily the thriller could edge towards tragic satire in our disordered times in which things fall apart, in which we seem more and more to be living in an 'Italian' society of the Jacobean kind. Today, as then, despite religious gloss on sentiment and language, we live in a world that is wholly secular, so that much official Christianity has a hollow, cynical ring. And the more the assumed, taken for granted moral values of a society become hollow and decay from within – rather than being challenged in a positive sense by an *alternative* system of values – the more that society becomes cynical, and the more it will rely on violence rather than reason to maintain the status quo. This, rather than Victorian values, is the meaning of the 'Thatcherism' which represents the modern in its most amoral form; commoditization, privatization, marketization, the promulgation of the view that money and profit constitute the *only* criteria for judging the value of anything, and the acceptance of the accompanying inevitable degradation with equanimity. Despite its authoritarianism, 'Thatcherism' represents an amoral order, in which the operations of the free market are treated more as though they were like the law of gravity than like Adam Smith's benign Hidden Hand, which was the hand of God. The authoritarianism is ultimately vacuous rather than morally committed authoritarianism (not that that makes it any less 'real'), a kind of *liberal* authoritarianism. And ironically, therefore, to the extent that 'Thatcherism' has succeeded in destroying the 'idea of socialism' (although to give Thatcherism the chief credit for that is to ignore too many other factors, the pusillanimity of the opposition included) the result has been to contribute to and intensify the decadence and 'anarchy' of the Thatcher world.

In this world the 'Italian-ness' is replaced by the 'American', the 'New York', even. The New York or Los Angeles of the American thriller is *our* moral dystopia, yet the place for which we most long, since it distils the essence of all our contradictions into one annihilating, yet beautiful, moment of perfect fear.

And in this world there can be, after all, no tragedy and no heroes. Nor can there, therefore, be villains. The chief protagonist of tragic satire unites the two roles in his one person. Yet it is not a case of good and evil struggling for his soul; that would give too much sense that things could have been otherwise than as they turn out; rather, he is a bystander at the events of his own life, like a picaresque hero he is more a field played upon by external forces, an accident waiting to happen, a mirror for a senseless world. Like an animal, he operates from instincts of self-preservation in a dangerous terrain, and like an animal he screams when hurt, yet he may as soon turn predator and close his jaws round a weaker victim in his way. A world, therefore, in which the actors act out of instinct, out of the unconscious, without much sense of choice, and therefore without much sense of morality. This is not the classic tragic hero at all – the great man brought low by one failing. Tragic satire is tragedy gone cold; violence steps in to substitute visceral for emotional responses. That is why

75

films are so violent; because the emotions to which they would once have sought to appeal have gone dead, or are an unknown quantity. Contemporary audiences often simply laugh at the violence.

Satire, whether comic or tragic, dehistoricizes the human attributes it mocks; these become timeless and unchanging, and this in turn leads to the fatalism of 'You can't change human nature' and to the acidity of stereotype and caricature. It is an ambiguous form, latently conservative in lacking a sense that things could be otherwise, or better; yet radical, too, even if only destructively, in attacking the powerful and their power, in denouncing the evil that men do, even if having no better moral universe to present as an alternative to the order that is mocked and derided. We are caught, with no way forward, and with nothing to believe in. This is neither tragic nor comic, but postmodern, deadpan satire.

This is all very well in theory; in practice even the most sophisticated audiences like characters with whom they can identify, or whom they can desire, people to 'care' about. The British film star Bob Hoskins has carried at least two films, *Mona Lisa* and *The Long Good Friday*, which ought to have qualified as 'tragic satire' or 'modern Jacobean', away from that genre by the force of his own personality. He was just too human, too lovable, too cuddly, for these would-be bleak films quite to bring off their vision of the dystopia that is contemporary Britain. The women in them – Helen Mirren and Kathie Tyson – had the right looks, beautiful in a desperate sort of way, and near the end of their tether, but the presence of Hoskins proved too conclusively that there is still good in the world. This good is personified by fat, short, 'ugly', but loyal and kindly men such as Hoskins, men who are no good in bed, or don't even get the chance, but who are solid, reliable and *there*. Another version of this character is Robbie Coltrane.

It is no accident that it is Kathie Tyson and not Bob Hoskins who shoots the villain in *Mona Lisa,* or that Hoskins and his daughter walk off into the sunset with Robbie Coltrane at the end of the film as a kind of reconstituted but asexual family; heading for some safe place. These films fell short of tragic satire, too, in their inability to create the tragically satirical woman. Kathie Tyson was too much of a victim and simply unconvincing as a doomed lesbian prostitute; Helen Mirren was motivelessly opaque.

Today's 'Jacobean' hero might be more like Stephen Ward of the Profumo Affair, a man without heroic qualities, brought down by forces that were stronger than he, his downfall implicit not in his character so much as in the world that created the character he was. For the protagonist of tragic satire can exist only in a special kind of world: a world like ours. Our world does, however, have affinities with the corrupt side of the fifties (although it lacks the vitality and the moral protest by which the fifties was redeemed). For, as today, the fifties – the early fifties, at least – mixed consumerism with bleakness; there was the Affluent Society, but there was the Bomb; there was the Cold War, but we'd never had it so good; there was more to eat, to drink, to do, and sex was beginning to come out of the closet; but the moral values were of another time, another place, a prewar suburb or an Edwardian villa; sex *was* still, often, secretive and shy, a fumbling with suspenders and condoms. (*Dance With A Stranger,* a film about Ruth Ellis, recreates that very well – most 'period' or pastiche films get it all wrong when it comes to 'period' sex.) It seemed as if all that had been got rid of in the sixties and seventies, but it's returned to haunt us, that terrible gloom, of pleasure linked with transgression (a very late-eighties word): back to sin, danger, outlawry, even if for different reasons.

We've hardly noticed that we live in a dystopia. In 1984 we congratulated ourselves that Orwell's dire vision *hadn't* come to pass. And yet in a way it has. In Orwell's novel, one of the cardinal features of the world he described was the public degradation of language; and in the contemporary use of language we can see how Orwell's future *is* with us, it has come true after all. We have failed to notice it because we are not all dressed in uniforms, nor do we live in a society in which sexuality is simply denied; but

77

the 'unspeak' is there – 'moderates', 'militants', 'loony left', 'Argies' and many, many others litter the pages of the mass media, words without real meaning other than as hate signals, code words for execration. Thus reasoned argument, and with it meaning, are destroyed. There is also the bureaucratized language of the DHSS communique, there is unspeakable academic prose, there is computer-speak, there is therapy-speak.

Then there are the proles, who, as in *1984*, are left to rot without too much attention being paid to their moral condition; they don't actually have to conform to the rules that constrict the 'flexible' working force. Soon all pretence will have been given up that the proles are ever going to get jobs, or that drug-addiction among them is under control. In fact, the tranquillizing and life-shortening properties of heroin will have turned out to be quite useful.

Of course there are differences. Life is more contradictory than any satire. In some ways our world more resembles Aldous Huxley's *Brave New World*, where banalized sex and technological birth are the norm. Moreover, the alternatives implied by Huxley and Orwell, and the focus of their moral denunciations, had implications that were ultimately conservative rather than progressive.

It may be, in any case, that it is wrong to think in terms of tragic satire at all. Possibly it is mistaken to conceptualize the contemporary hero in terms of downfall, destruction and doom. Maybe the heroes of today are those whose downfall does not lead to downfall, who with bland, cardboard smiles rise again and carry on as though nothing had happened; Cecil Parkinson or Jeffrey Archer, perhaps. A truly postmodern alternative to the Jacobean fall guy, this. No tragedy, no satire, not even farce, but only smiling blandness, Cheshire-cat smiles.

12

Cabaret

Downstairs, the main bars are oak-panelled and chintzy, an incongruously home-counties interior for a very mixed crowd of locals, neither trendy nor especially well-heeled. The punters are crowding in, and with their drinks they walk up some outside stairs, across a flat roof and into a dimly lit room with a dais at the far end, some tables and chairs set out in front of it and space round the back and sides for the late-comers who will have to stand. At five to nine it's still half empty, but by the time the first act is through the place is jammed. For this is cabaret night at the Cricklewood Hotel in Brent, north-west London.

In this upstairs room the crowd is more homogeneous than the downstairs clientele: mostly between the ages of (roughly) twenty-five and thirty-five, women and men in more or less equal numbers, and several groups of women on their own. On this particular occasion – just before the 1987 General Election – we catch a glimpse of Ken Livingstone himself, Labour candidate and soon to be Labour MP for Brent East, enjoying the show and happy to take the credit for the funding of the venue by the Greater London Council before its demise, a successful, and typical example of the GLC Arts Policy.

On this night as on others the show follows an established pattern. First there is always an unknown, and the female commere tells us that if we give him a big clap he'll get asked to come again – a nice example of the delicate power balance between audience and acts, for these debutante stand-up comics are usually inhibited by lack of confidence, their nervousness prevents the jokes from getting across, and sometimes the buzz of chatter threatens cruelly to sink these hopeful young men, who look like pre-war schoolboys in their uniform chic of slicked-back hair and white shirts and square-shouldered jackets, and who dream of making the leap from dole queue to small screen by way of the tawdry chic of alternative cabaret.

It's these openers that depend most strongly either on straightforward filth or else on a vein of bodily disgust. One boy we've seen once or twice has developed a rich monologue on the horror of bodily functions in which maggots, genitals, sweat and body hair mingle so forcefully that you can almost smell his act, it gives off the rank, seedy, but also Armani stink of Thatcher's Britain.

On any given evening there's likely to be a magician or juggler. These, even if, as usually is the case, they keep up a satirical running commentary as they perform, appeal primarily to the more innocent and childlike aspect of the audience. It's refreshing on a Friday night to gaze wide-eyed as a pigeon flutters from a hat or someone swallows an egg only to produce it from his pocket the next moment. A fire-eater provokes only half-joking cries of 'What about the fire regulations?' yet the frisson of genuine alarm as smoke and flame swirls in the direction of the GLC banner at the back of the stage is balanced by the reassuring knowledge that this *is* all make-believe, that it's all all right, nothing's going to go wrong.

Yet there is a hint of sadism, that balancing of hostility and benevolence, exploited by performers and audience alike. Integral to cabaret is the convention whereby the comics will choose a butt, and the performers an assistant from the audience. Better not to sit too near the front if you're self-conscious about looking 'like a prat' as one victim put it. Sometimes the unfortunate individual singled out will be allowed to remain in his seat and will simply have vaguely threatening remarks addressed to him by a performer (or if he's really unlucky, by a succession of them).

'What's your name? Yes, *you*. Oh – Rick – I see. *Rick*. You stick to one syllable, do you, Rick. I see. Okay ... And what do you do, for a living I mean, Rick? Rick? You look like a *supply teacher* to me, yes ... and what is that you're wearing, Rick? A symphony in beige, I think ...'

A little later, just as Rick thinks he's been thankfully forgotten, it will be:

'Well, did you enjoy that Rick? You're looking a bit nervous ...'

As well Rick might.

Occasionally it is the performer who has the worst of it. On one occasion at the Cricklewood Hotel a charmingly laid-back juggler invited a woman onto the platform to assist him with some of his tricks (although 'invite' is not quite the right word on these occasions). She quickly upstaged him, insisting on balancing a glass of wine on her forehead while lowering herself to the ground with great aplomb, introduced a rival line in badinage, and finally announced herself as the author of a book on horoscopes, which could be purchased at Compendium Books, Camden Town.

More often it is the luckless invitee who is browbeaten into participating in a series of events in which he (it does more often seem to be a he) is made to look mildly ridiculous, but which earns him the tolerant affection of the audience, who will sometimes protest if the professional is too rude about his 'assistant'. The other function of the stooge is to point up the absurdity of the performance itself. A female fire-eater at the Hackney Empire, who also went in for extremely vigorous belly-dancing, forced her chosen partner to recline on the stage in a silver lamé skirt while she jumped and thumped round him, finally forcing a bar of Turkish delight between his teeth in a raucous parody of the erotic. Similarly the conjuror's assistants are there in part to contribute to the atmosphere of parody, these performances being in part a critique of their own genre.

But sometimes the tables are turned and someone, or, more threateningly a group, turns nasty. This happened once at the Cricklewood Hotel, when a knot of local lads near the bar refused to stop talking, and began seriously to annoy the artistes. The laid-back juggler merely resorted to his own running commentary – 'Has the jury reached a verdict yet?' and so on – but the next performer, a fragile-looking female comic, objected in forceful terms. The talking turned to heckling, whereupon she advanced menacingly towards the group, shouting abuse. For a moment things got really tense as she yelled:

'You guys, *get off*! I do my act like you have sex: ALONE!'

But the moment of aggro passed. And anyway, for the rest of the audience it seemed to be part of the fun, as they watched impartially, waiting to see who would win.

The best performers are those who have developed a complete stage personality, with props, catch-phrases and an at times surreal form of humour which goes beyond the satire of even the sharpest comics to create a kind of fantasy world-turned-upside-down which holds a wildly distorting mirror to the common-sense, taken-for-granted assumptions of daily life. One such is Frederick Benson, who comes on made-up like Frankenstein's monster in a lamé jacket and works up an atmosphere of disconnected farce; another is the Joan Collins Fan Club, whose co-star is Fanny the Wonder Dog.

On the night Ken Livingstone graced the Cricklewood Hotel the final act was rather different: the dub poet Benjamin Zephaniah. A slender man with long dreadlocks, his slight smile and slow, rocking to and fro movements lull the audience into a warm sense of rapport and at the same time become slightly sinister when he chants his poems about police beatings and interrogations and life in a Borstal. The laughter he generates is grimmer, more serious than that which greets his fellow performers, for his is a genuinely political performance. He is also unusual on the cabaret circuit in being black.

Even at the Hackney Empire the cabaret audience has – when I have been there, anyway – been almost exclusively white middle class. The Hackney Empire is a red and gilt music hall with fake marbling in the foyer and Ottoman domes above the boxes in the auditorium. Its revitalization for the 1980s is consistent with the gentrification of parts of Hackney itself. The Stoke Newington district in particular is being colonized by social workers and others who value the area for its link with a radical past and with a working-class history or way of life that hovers like an aura over Stoke Newington Church Street. (Their presence has also to do, of course, and most importantly, with property values and changing mortgage practices by the building societies and banks.) But an imagined past does not quite fit with the present reality of life for the black and white working class in the inner city. Patrick White in his essay 'The ghosting of the inner city' in *On Living in an Old Country* muses on this postmodern re-creation of a romanticized, slightly fake past: 'Stoke Newington is not so much a literal place as a cultural oscillation between the prosaic reality of the contemporary inner city and an imaginative reconstruction of the past.'[1] While he admits to being a resident himself, there is an also rather postmodern disavowal and detachment in his commentary, as though he, by virtue of his perceptive analysis, is absolved from complicity in the gentrification process of which he is actually a part. But this is a rather characteristic response of the 'progressive' gentrifiers, whose intellectual understanding of the changes going on in the inner city, of which they *are* a part, is split; they both perceive the disadvantages to others and appreciate the benefits to themselves, yet to bring the two together would generate guilt, so different perceptions exist, and have to remain hysterically separated.

For this group, anyway, the Hackney Empire represents an authentic form of working-class culture, and the regeneration of this particular music hall saves both the theatre itself and a part of local past history for the people of Hackney. Yet it is the more recent Hackney residents rather than the inner-city working class for whom the Empire seeems to cater; it achieves an alternative rather than a local audience.

This audience loved the Joan Collins Fan Club as he stalked the stage in costumes that combined the extremes of masculinity and femininity in one (black leather body suit under a filmy red negligée). Here at least the gay identity isn't on the run, is celebrated in uncompromising terms with defiance and a hectoring mastery over the audience.

Both the camp presence and the jokes about Chief Constable Anderton represent 'anti-Thatcherism': the dislike of hypocrisy, of the status quo and of the conservatism of establishment 'morality' and establishment politics which are hallmarks of alternative humour. It feels like a return to what one imagines the 1920s in central Europe was like, when the avant garde used 'decadence' and outrage as critiques of the existing order. But this critical spirit can come close to nihilism if it lacks a clear position of its own from which to mount its attack. Maybe this negativism on both sides of the proscenium explains the tension between audience and performers, the four-letter words and body-hating jokes, the spectacle that borders from time to time on psychological sadism. Gay outrage is particularly well suited to this iconoclastic ambience. On the other hand the persistence of a strong gay cultural presence in the face of rising anti-gay hysteria is due to, and also gives it, a more cutting political edge. The gays, like the blacks, have an identifiable, and threatened community, and you can't be black or gay without knowing very clearly who the enemy is; whereas the white radicals often seem to be all over the place.

Gay outrage in cabaret is not about sex so much as about gender politics. Homosexuality can seem like the most flaunting of all forms of rejection of the common sense of a scared, cowed and shabby society. If the 'natural' heterosexual coupling isn't sacred, then what on earth can be? Camp is the least utopian of 'alternative' attitudes, often more like a jarring, jeering 'No' to every social imperative, every suggestion that there is anything but humbug in society's norms. As the Joan Collins Fan Club says of his own act, 'it's uncanny and unnatural'. The atmosphere of Joe Orton's plays is similar; manic iconoclasm destroys every decency; corpses and naughty nighties, false teeth and mistaken identity, false pretences and colostomy bags are flung together on the same level of horror/absurdity, an abolition of the whole hierarchy of the social universe, an avant garde postmodernist juxtaposition of the non-related which gives people the jitters.

Yet although it subverts all categories of the normal, how subversive is camp, even in the current political climate? If you are not careful it can seem like just a prank, if you are not careful it can merely mirror the often forced or senseless juxtapositions of the consumer world. 'Although irony,' comments Franco Moretti, 'is an indispensable component of any critical, democratic and progressive culture, its modernist version has a dark side,'[2] and he goes on to argue that its ambiguity may be so great as to lead to a cultural and political irresponsibility; irony can easily undercut any or all committed positions. It comes from nowhere; shaking the contents of the society of the spectacle as if in a kaleidoscope it creates a new pattern but still within the mirrored tube.

In the interval of the Joan Collins Fan Club extravaganza my companion and I wondered at the reasons for the resurgence of this cultural form – cabaret – as the eighties edges towards the nineties. In one way it is consistent with the Thatcherist emphasis on the small enterprise. Although some of the venues may be funded by local authorities, the performers are self-generated, creatures of the recession, like cocktail-bar pianists and nannies (we thought all those callings were extinct with the thirties), and to get into the cabaret circuit is, if you like, a new form of petty commodity capitalism, it's the lumpen intelligentsia living on its wits and at the same time hanging on to at least the possibility of saying 'No' while surviving through the hard times: a displaced politics outside the political sphere. The values are anti-capitalist, yet their expression is part of the capitalism of the inner-city wastes, those forlorn regions recolonized with a few tender flowers among the corrugated iron fencing: here a wine bar, there a boutique, again an ethnic restaurant or a homeopathy clinic. It's the anything goes, anarchic side of capitalism, who cares what it says, there's a profit there for someone, not so much for the designers, the performers, the chefs, as for the property developers – the invisible face of capitalism.

And yet, as we hung over the balcony at the back of the stalls in the interval (and this was the evening after the day

on which Parliament had decided to pass an amendment to
the Local Government Bill which makes it illegal for local
authorities to 'promote' homosexuality) my friend said:

'Of course they had cabaret in the Weimar Republic,
didn't they. Before the Nazis.'

13

Money

I always seem to have less money than other people – or else much more. Out there are the grotesque disparities that I can't even imagine – between the beggars along the High Road whose requests for money have become so routine you hardly even notice, and the city millionaires a few miles further up the hill.

But closer to home (even closer to home) even my peers seem to operate at a different level from me. They surround themselves with machines, for a start. Microwaves have followed word-processors, which came after – was it dish-washers or clothes driers; videos, maybe. Anyway, the epoch when household machinery consisted of a hoover, a washing machine and a fridge (not even a telly) are long gone; now there's a forest of plastic hardware which is supposed to give you the free time to do those 'other things' your mother only dreamed about when lighting the fires or sweeping the stairs in those houses with no central heating and no fully-fitted kitchen to minimize her toil. (Then, the only fully-fitted things were stockings, and she took hours getting the seams straight.) Of course, as a friend remarked, it is nice to sit in your kitchen and listen to your machines humming away and doing the work for you, although, as another friend (female, of course) also remarked, the coming of the word-processor just means a whole new series of horrible ways to spend a Saturday morning, toiling up and down the Tottenham Court Road in search of a solution to the mystery of why it's gone wrong again. On the other hand, if my friends are to be believed, the word-processor *is* in a class of its own. What they *say* is, 'It moves whole paragraphs around.' (Why would you want to do *that*?) They always seem, however, to be implying that what it actually does is *write whole books by itself*. My scepticism feels like a form of vanity, an obsessional insistence on the importance of my own individual input.

Machines are wonderful, then – maybe – but they are also boring – or is that just my feminine socialization again. Certainly, I always used to imagine that what I would buy for my house when I had enough money was Persian carpets, paintings, beautiful antique furniture. Alas, this is an essentially nineteenth-century concept of the ideal interior, displaced today by the more modern and less élitist idea of comfort. An interior to reflect one's personality, taste and level of education seems egotistical, ostentatious, undemocratic; the avoidance of discomfort a more egalitarian goal, since it implies neither aesthetic snobbery nor a regrettably Eurocentric standard of taste.

The many holidays other people take seem more directly enviable. (How can they afford *three*?) But again, I discover I'm locked in a student past, my ideal simply to take off without either preparation or luggage, it's a cop-out to book even a single night in a hotel in advance. I should have discovered the package, another egalitarian mode: 'It's perfectly all right, you don't have to *do* anything when you get there, just a flight and a hotel.'

Then there are even those, among these radical friends, who are talking of public school (especially for boys, one is not very surprised to notice). Now I *am* horrified. Quite apart from the political meaning of this, don't they cost hundreds of pounds a term? And then there are personal services: therapists, daily helps, nannies, homeopathic healers.

Now I myself have either had recourse to some of these or can at least understand the anxieties that may lead to the adoption of remedies as desperate as public schools. But on the one hand I always discover that I cannot afford any of these 'necessities' (try explaining to your bank manager why you *have* to spend £100 a week on psychoanalysis) – so how do the others manage; and on the other hand there is a sense of being swept away in a tide of change that is neither actively desired nor wholly understood.

The question of nannies and home helps seems to be particularly contentious, and is noticeably more likely to be condemned by radical *men*. But what else are professional or other relatively high-earning women with children to do if, as is usually the case, their male partners are still shouldering very much less than half the burden of domestic labour? The relatively few women who qualify for a secretary of their own at work don't feel this is wrong, and perhaps the same argument should apply to domestic help, although the opportunities for exploitation are greater. It is a murky area, and one in which women on both sides may feel ill at ease with the inequality of the relationship. It reflects changes in the position of women in ways that were not anticipated in 1970, and some of the response explicitly from feminists illustrates the way in which what may be loosely called a 'Thatcherist' ideology has permeated even what remains of the women's movement.

For example in one Inner London Local Authority, the Women's Unit – set up to promote equal opportunities for women – has never been supportive of the workplace nursery which was set up with the backing of the trade union, on the grounds that it is 'élitist' in offering childcare to 'middle-class' women (although in fact *any* woman employed by the Council was entitled to a nursery place). This workerist attitude has the most reactionary implications. Even if a very few women achieve positions of responsibility, and good salaries through their own endeavours at work, thus creating a tiny 'élite' of women in employment, we should surely support rather than condemn them, while to pioneer workplace nurseries makes it easier for *all* women to undertake paid work. In any case, the idea that 'privileged' women don't deserve nursery places, suggests *either* that they should resort to the private market in childcare – thus creating further inequalities and worse conditions of work, on the whole, for the nannies and childminders who are such an exploitable section of the workforce; *or* that these 'privileged' women should not be at work at all – that a mother's place is, after all, in the home. This is the Thatcherist policy of charity, of provision for the needy only, whereas we all know that it is only universal services that avoid stigma and the connotations of a second-class service for those who are too shiftless or stupid (as this argument implies) to provide for themselves.

None the less, the women who twenty years ago were beginning to create the movement for women's liberation would have been *horrified* to be told that what the future held in store was an even more divided female workforce, in which there are more and more low-paid, casualized women workers. A new servant class is being created from this pool of labour; hardly what was envisaged in the brave days of sisterhood and utopian socialism. But it is unfair and unreasonable to blame the few women who do manage to get relatively well-paid and secure jobs for this parlous state of affairs.

In just such ways, though, is the ground breaking up under our feet and the landscape disintegrating around us. But if a small group of women now in middle age have to some extent been the unexpected beneficiaries – or have at least hung in there – there are those, only a few years younger who, despite the privilege of education, seem permanently condemned to a lumpen-intelligentsia existence of part-time work, freelancing precariously, living from hand to mouth on odd lectures, temporary administrative jobs, the one-off consultancy. The free market in cultural production operates as capriciously and dangerously as it does in services and the finance sector. No wonder that some of these polytechnic temps – if they are women – may find in more traditional forms of marriage and childrearing than feminists in the 1970s would have endorsed (in public at least) an economic solution to an existence that would otherwise be as drab as that of the Gissing heroines of the 1890s. The unanchored, unmarried woman writer or journalist living on her wits faces just as uncertain a future today as did her forebears a hundred years ago. What George Gissing wrote about in *The Odd Women* is echoed today in Rebecca O'Rourke's *Jumping the Cracks*, in which the heroine 'owns' her marginalized identity with a mixture of bitterness and pride. Once married, on the other hand (provided her husband has a few bob), a woman may devote much of her time to writing novels or engaging in other rewarding but unremunerative activities.

Winifred Holtby, an unmarried, and possibly lesbian, feminist of the 1930s, voiced her unease at this solution in that earlier period of economic depression and right-wing politics:

Too many ... women use the domestic tradition to evade responsibility for everything else ... finding it easier to be a good housewife than a good citizen. So long as their own children are healthy and happy, why worry because others are ill and frightened? It is agreeable to distemper one's own nursery, bake crusts, squeeze oranges and mix nourishing salads; it is not agreeable to sit on quarrelling committees, listen to tedious speeches, organise demonstrations and alter systems, in order that others – for whom such wholesome pleasures are at present impossible – may enjoy them.[1]

I have often quoted this passage, for its uncompromising acknowledgement of the avenues of retreat into the private that are usually open to the more privileged women in our society. Of course women should have the opportunity to develop their creativity, but this does not absolve them from public responsibility.

It is not women only, however, who may turn their backs on the traditional work ethic altogether. The government and the DHSS always fear what does in some cases happen to the long-term unemployed: they adopt non-consumerist values (though these may be consistent with activity in what is called euphemistically the 'informal economy').

This is an area about which, for obvious reasons, we can officially know relatively little, in the sense that individuals may be shy of divulging their actual patterns of work to researchers and statisticians, for fear that the tax collector may appear in the researcher's wake. Ray Pahl[2] managed to do some research in this area on the Isle of Sheppey in the late 1970s. He suggests that there are many different patterns of work, but that there may be an increasing polarization between households where there are no earners, and those with two or multiple earners. It does not necessarily follow that it is in the former that domestic labour will fill the empty hours that were once devoted to paid work, since there may be no money for the wherewithal to redecorate, cook or sew. On the other hand the two-earner household may make use of the proliferating services such as fast food take-aways, commercial cleaning services and entertainment ouside the home. Other households, however, either because of poverty *or* for the opposite reason undertake activities such as baking their own bread, making their own clothes and performing other 'creative' work that enhances their 'lifestyle'. In areas such as parts of Belfast where unemployment is an almost universal condition the means of cultural and psychological survival may extend to publicly provided educational and leisure facilities: the unemployed study for O levels, A levels and degrees, take courses in foreign languages, art and anthropology; they exercise fanatically to a pitch of condition, become the chess or karate 'stars' of this alternative society. The only problem is they lack the money to achieve even the minimum standards of comfort. Self-education and self-improvement are admirable; yet in some ways this way of life reminds me of the long-term prisoners described by Paul Walton[3] and others. These category A criminals were getting through their thirty-year sentences in similar ways – two hundred press-ups a day and the Open University course were their lifebelts for survival, and with which they blocked the view of a future of terrifying sameness stretching before them with no promise, ever, of any change or improvement in their environment. And chronic unemployment is a form of imprisonment too – with the difference that it is visited on those who have committed no crime.

These different ways of life are difficult to reach and to know. Journalistic and popular cultural attempts to pin them down seem usually to result in caricature. For example, critics – including those of the *New Socialist* and

MONEY

City Limits – loved the 1987 film *Rita Sue and Bob Too* for its 'realistic' portrayal of post-industrial northern life.

The story is a simple one: Rita and Sue are school friends, who get a job baby-sitting for a nouveau-riche couple. The husband, Bob, drives them home, but makes a detour to the moors, where he deflowers both of them, to their apparent delight. (It is by no means clear that these girls have reached the age of consent.) The seduction scene is played as grittily realistic – 'rubber johnnies' are discussed and dangled around; the sexual act is filmed unromantically. But in fact the film is pure fantasy. Critics may have perceived 'realism' in the shots of a poverty-stricken housing estate; this was just a gloss of pseudo-realism on a scenario of pure wish-fulfilment. Rita's biker brothers; the family row in front of the flats, watched by neighbours; the sexual distaste of the nouveau-riche couple; all these are just stereotypic jokes from which the real pain of poverty is drained away, the real fear of aggression and violence banished. Instead, the underclass in its squalid yet – in a new urban way – picturesque 'reservations' is rendered as a simply rather lovable part of the contemporary landscape.

Even more offensively, the real unpleasantness of the spectacle of a middle-aged man running two schoolgirls is sweetened by blaming his wife. (How old-fashioned can you get!) She is portrayed – and one-dimensionally acted – as a complete bitch, for reasons the film never bothers to explore. On the other hand the triangular relationship is implicitly justified by the fact that the girls are shown as being even keener on their ageing lover than he is on them; another case of wish-fulfilment, presumably, on behalf of men in the audience. Bob's sexual exploits, the film implies, are positively heroic, and at the close of the film the three of them have set up a *ménage à trois* (an untimely pregnancy having conveniently aborted itself).

That this is little more than a rather dishonest version of the 'Carry On' series, updated for the 1980s – *Carry On On the Social*, perhaps – is signalled by the banality of the visual jokes. For example there is the tedious running gag

93

of the neighbour, who watches the high jinks while watering his garden; time and again we return to the same shot of this character with his hose, prurience, astonishment and so on being signalled by how many yards in the wrong direction his jet of water is directed.

If this is one popular portrait of Thatcher's Britain, another is much more skilfully deployed by Nicholas Coleridge in the glossy magazine *Harper's Queen*. In a series of vignettes, which seem to focus particularly on women, he describes the lives of the more-or-less upper-class young: daughters who become the mistresses of men old enough to be their fathers; Chelsea hustlers on the fringes of the art or media world; young male workaholics who are bored by sex; women coining money in the city, and their 'poor' cousins who make a living by camping in houses they do up, sell for a vast profit and move on. These Sloanes, making out on credit cards instead of social security, like to read books such as Tamar Janovitz's *Slaves of New York*, or the bizarre neurological case histories gathered together by Oliver Sacks in *The Man Who Mistook his Wife for a Hat* – reading matter which reflects the fragmentary quality of their own lives. For them, too, everything is provisional and dislocated, nothing really leads anywhere, they're waiting for something to turn up.

These are random examples of the way in which an image of Thatcher's 'post-industrial' Britain is culturally constructed. But, as Ray Pahl's research suggests, there is another side to the story: the *re-industrialization* of Britain along new and more authoritarian lines. His first visit to the Isle of Sheppey revealed a whole variety of creative efforts in the home assisted by various methods of augmented supplementary benefit, not excluding large-scale pilfering from the docks, with stories of crates of oranges and even whole sheep, that mysteriously went missing. Although unemployment was already high, there were still plenty of men and women in work, the dock stevedores in particular earning comparatively high wages, and this meant that there were opportunities for 'informal' work – that is, those in formal employment could afford to pay others to carry out services such as car-tuning and interior decoration while still claiming benefit. In some cases, on the other hand, such services were bartered, thereby avoiding both tax evasion and DHSS fraud.

However, when Ray Pahl returned in 1981, five years after his initial visit, things had changed. Unemployment had risen to such an extent that few could afford the luxuries from the docks and had become resentful of those who had made most money from those activities; there was less money all round to pay for 'informal' services; the police had clamped down. Most importantly, a new motor assembly factory had come to the island, replacing the goods previously handled at the docks; dock security had been tightened; a new industrial discipline was being imposed; the remains of the tourist industry had declined, since by the 1980s anyone who could afford a holiday at all was sufficiently well off to go somewhere better than the Isle of Sheppey. The hatches had been battened down.

So, many patterns emerge. The almost idyllic view of contemporary English life found in *Rita Sue and Bob Too*, which turns urban squalor into another romantic aspect of 'our heritage' or that in *Harper's Queen* which emphasizes the *apparent* rootlessness of the upper-class young, occludes other lives and other communities: the mining communities around the new 'super mines'; the women workers in the proliferating inner-city sweat-shops; the 'progressive' private sector of social workers turned therapists, of white-collar trades unionists turned managers. These latter seem sometimes to have forgotten that their original purpose in the public sector was to provide educational, health or social *services*, and to have adopted enthusiastically the cost-cutting values of central government. Theirs is but one example, no doubt, of the ways in which we all seek to give our lives meaning, to believe in and to justify that which we are paid to do.

For money is a medium in which we look at ourselves 'through a glass, darkly' and not 'face to face'. We need it so much that surely whatever we do to get it *must* be moral, must be virtuous, must be right. So if money is the measure of all things, if, as Georg Simmel wrote, it reduces everything else to its indifferent and amoral self, then also it may place *any* activity in the flattering light of that which is positively enjoined. If they pay you to do it, it *must* be all right to do.

14

Second-hand Films

'There's more of women than anything in the world – except insects.'

Johnny Farrell in Gilda

'I didn't see *Gilda*, the film everyone was talking about,' wrote Simone de Beauvoir[1] of the year 1947. What did they say about *Gilda* in Paris in the austerity years? Fascinated by all things American – America, the land of modernity, the land of optimism – de Beauvoir might have enjoyed it as she enjoyed Hemingway, Chandler. But she could not have enjoyed it as *film noir*, for that category had not yet been invented.

The contemporary appreciation of this genre of forty-year-old black and white films is akin to our recent love of second-hand clothing, the 'forties frocks' we loved in the seventies. And indeed, just as the clothing industry rushed out pastiche copies of those little puff-sleeved, printed crêpe numbers, so the film industry has attempted to create anew the *film noir* – with *Body Heat*, a remake of *Double Indemnity*, for example, or the remakes of *The Postman Always Rings Twice* and *Farewell My Lovely*, the latter complete with one of the great *noir* stars, Robert Mitchum himself. But the films, like the dresses, are not so easily re-invented. A new imitation is not the same as the old real thing.

We respond aesthetically to retro chic or thrift shop clothes in oblique ways, and the pleasure we take in them is hard to pin down. In the first place they are a little uncanny, having belonged to women who are now probably dead; these clothes have inhabited another world, when we were children, or before we were born, but by dressing up in them (and it is in part a child's game of dressing up) we may ourselves imaginatively enter that lost world. Yet simultaneously these garments act to distance us from that other time, marking our own knowing sophistication about the ironies and self-importance of self-adornment, while rendering it more respectable, in that in taking on the dress codes of another era we reclaim an hitherto unappreciated aspect of the past. A re-evaluation occurs and is inscribed upon our persons, thus signalling our refinement and advanced taste. This sort of dressing renounces *obvious* sex appeal, glamour and smartness in favour of a dated chic that openly evokes the poignancy of the ephemeral.[2]

Film noir works in a similar way. The period ambience distances us from the narrative; it is that much less easy for us to identify with the main characters, and correspondingly the absurdities of plot and character are glaringly obvious. *Gilda*, for example, is full of gaping holes in credibility, sudden reversals in plot and changes in personality that we cannot take seriously. A happy ending is tacked on which makes nonsense of the relationship between Gilda and her lover, Johnny, for the whole point of the relationship was its doomed, love/hate quality – until the last reel. But our awareness of the 'trash' aspect of such films reinforces our sense of our own sophistication, as we – whether consciously or not – compare ourselves with the original audience of the then new film.

Everything that this film has to say about love is never expressed, yet is powerfully present in the strange, triangular relationship between Ballen, the benefactor, and his two protégées. The film begins as he 'saves' the down-and-out Johnny, who rapidly becomes his right-hand man in the gambling club he owns. The psychoanalytic sequence is reversed, for in this family, Johnny's first parent is Ballen, the father, who grants him a rebirth as his henchman. Ballen possesses a swordstick, which acts as the 'third term' in their relationship – Ballen openly refers to the weapon as completing the triangle ('Just the three of us, Johnny'). Unexpectedly, however, he returns from one of his journeys away accompanied by Gilda. Although Ballen does not know this, Gilda and Johnny have been lovers in some shadowy former existence that is never elucidated; but in any case 'just the three of us' now takes on a different meaning with the entry of this threateningly seductive 'mother'. Johnny is the Oedipal child torn between love/hate for each partner in the heterosexual parental couple. He is the tolerated 'safe' intruder in the marital bedroom, and indeed Ballen consigns Gilda to Johnny's care. On the one hand masculinity is a homoerotic pact in which a woman may represent a phallus, yet on the other hand this very pact suggests the castration of Johnny, since he *is* regarded as 'safe'.

As we react 'knowingly' to the general exaggerations and absurdities of *film noir*, so do we also react to the 'unconscious' homosexual undertones in *Gilda*. Although it appears that the cast were themselves aware of the deviant construction that could be placed on the relationship between Johnny and Ballen[3], I believe that the 'sophisticated' reaction of today's audience is based on an assumption of the innocence of that earlier audience, who took at face value what we read as outrageously camp.

Not that *Gilda* is a camp experience; although we may enjoy the over-the-top aspect of Rita Hayworth's femme fatale, our engagement with the film is more complex. *Sunset Boulevard* is camp at times – with the cruelty towards women of camp – in showing us the spectacle of Gloria Swanson caricaturing herself as an ageing megalomaniac film star from the silent era. But both Gilda herself and the Johnny/Ballen relationship are treated romantically. It is the old romance of thwarted or forbidden love, with the added ambiguity that Johnny (Glenn Ford) is in some ways positioned as feminine in the triangular relationship.[4] For much of the film it is passion as hatred that is celebrated, all three characters expressing their love or obsession in acts or words of sadism – Gilda even appears dressed for the carnival in an Argentinian costume with boots, a cowboy hat and a whip. Surrender on the other hand – even if it is Gilda begging to be *released* from her marriage to Johnny, when she actually kneels and clasps his legs – is equated with masochism. The surface exaggerations and absurdities, the *decadence*, in a way, of the film, cannot muffle, and perhaps even enhances, the power of these compulsive attractions, and touch a chord, perhaps unacknowledged, in the audience.

The feminist interpretation of *film noir* is to emphasize the contradictory role played by women in these narratives: portrayed as powerful, threatening, independent and downright evil, yet 'recuperated' and placed back securely 'in the end' within the safe confines of marriage and family (as in *Mildred Pierce*), or righteously killed off. The feminist gloss on *Gilda* in addition makes much of the famous sequence in which Rita Hayworth, the 'great star', the 'love goddess', sings the brash, bold 'Put the blame on Mame' – certainly a song with a feminist message: when-ever anything in the world goes wrong, men 'put the blame on Mame'. Of course this message is undercut by Rita Hayworth's appearance, in tight, strapless black evening dress and long black gloves which she strips off in a gesture both defiant and provocative, yet this flaunting sexuality is also interpreted as demonstrating freedom and a glorious acknowledgement of her own sexuality. She is, it is true, not quite the typical *film noir* heroine, too beautiful, or beautiful in the wrong way, a beauty that makes her more vulnerable and less menacing than the strange, cold looks of a Joan Crawford or a Barbara Stanwyck, but as Richard Dyer points out, it's not exactly an image of women's liberation.

To Ballen, the sadist as Nazi (for such he turns out to be) is given the role of suppressed (cold) and therefore more threatening sexual being, while in the closing scenes of the film Gilda becomes another child, a sister, a comrade (although a lover too, at last) to Johnny – or the mother who sides definitively with the child – in throwing off, with him, the domination of the patriarchal Ballen: pure Oedipal wish-fulfilment. This links back to the carniva-lesque scene in which the guests at Ballen's nightclub celebrate the defeat of Germany which is also the moment at which Ballen knows he will have to leave.

Yet male vulnerability still haunts the margins of this picture, which hints at the paradoxical Achilles heel in the contemporary construction of the masculine: that either to love (to experience desire) *or* to be its (implicitly passive) object is to suggest an unacceptable, even an unmentionable weakness. In this *film noir* at least, contrary to the more usual interpretations, the dangers of loving Gilda, the dangers of female sexuality, are shown as less dangerous than the dangers of the depths of love between men. But hence also the falsity of the film's 'happy' ending, which denies what the film itself has demonstrated: that Johnny is caught between the devil and the deep blue sea, that there is no solution.

One of the pleasures of *film noir* is the visual, especially in two respects: the expressionism of the dark/light contrasts; and the Art Deco or otherwise 'thirties' or modernist appearance of buildings and interiors, including location shots of parts of Los Angeles and Southern California that no longer exist save in this ghostly celluloid form. In *The Big Sleep*, *Cat People* and *Dark Passage* (and many other films) there are wonderful shots of deco staircases and Hollywood lounges: in *Cat People* the eerie swimming pool, in *Dark Passage* a beautiful moment when you watch the ascent of a lift up a glass shaft outside a modernist apartment block. Again, the aesthetic effect of this is the 'double-take' of experiencing as 'period' what originally constructed itself as 'modern', as 'the latest thing'.

Dark Passage is a less well-known film than *Gilda*, and is a story of a different type. Its heroine is supportive and subordinate, although the moral standing and veracity of the hero, like that of Johnny in *Gilda*, is unstable and in doubt. He is an escapee from Alcatraz (which in itself stretches credibility). Managing to leave the prison island in a dustcart, he hides in a ditch and then thumbs a lift from a young woman artist (Lauren Bacall). His crime was to have murdered his lover, yet although Bacall soon guesses his identity, she never for a moment doubts his innocence. On the contrary, she hides him in her apartment and helps him to get to an underworld doctor who alters his face.

Until the point at which the bandages are removed, the audience never sees the hero; every shot is as seen by him, from behind his eyes, as it were, although we know that he has the voice of Humphrey Bogart. When the bandages are removed to reveal the hero's 'new' face – that is, he has 'become' Bogart – the effect is ambiguous and unsettling, because we also know that he must have 'been' Bogart all along. This makes us even less certain of his identity as hero or villain.

The evil woman does appear in this film, in the person of Agnes Moorhead. The friend of the murdered woman, and also of Lauren Bacall, she discovers his presence in the flat, accuses him again of the murder and then throws herself out of the window to her death. Thus he will be incriminated of this new 'crime', which will be construed as murder.

Yet the narrative insists on his innocence, and although the police net draws more and more closely round this paranoid innocent, miraculously he makes his escape in the teeth of the manhunt, jumping aboard the bus to Mexico as the cops frisk passengers in the bus station. The closing frames of the film show him in dinner jacket in a Latin American resort, as he rises to greet Lauren Bacall, who has arrived to be reunited with him. Is this a dream ending or is it real?

So, like *Gilda, Dark Passage* is simultaneously a work of pure wish-fulfilment, the triumph of the pleasure principle, and a film which expresses the fears to which the 'dream' is the fantasy solution. But the dream of a happy ending never manages to cancel out the fears, in this case fear embodied as a shadowed vision of urban life as persecution and danger, a nightmare of lost or threatened identity. The prisoner on the run cannot be what he is, cannot perform on the city stage, can only exist lost in its interstices.

Although in many *films noirs* the resolution restores 'normality' (for example in *Double Indemnity* in a very clear way, with the villainness shot dead by her lover, who then himself has to die, so that the 'badness' has been removed from the world) the 'happier' endings are remarkably unsatisfactory. The normal and cheerful remains the unreal. In *Cat People*, the catwoman, played by the beautiful Simone Simon – a film star with a face like a cat – has to die, yet the hero mourns her integrity ('she never lied'), and his prosaic, normal girlfriend seems brisk and unromantic by comparison. The normality and safety of the professor's family in *Woman in the Window* is tedious and stale, yet his erotic life, which in any case exists only in his dream, is so dangerous that it leads to murder.[5] There is no third way between the deadly decadence of erotic love and the dismal reality of domestic life. There *is* no solution.

Film noir is explained in terms of urban angst, the postwar social unease of late forties America. But why should it appeal to us today? The 'rediscovery' of the genre suggests that we have come to have a special liking for flawed, dislocated art works. The genre has, in fact, been not so much rediscovered as created out of our sensibility, an intellectual sensibility, it seems, which values most that art which is most in need of elucidation and interpretation, the work that most includes us. We enjoy, also, the nostalgic dream of imagining that we are back in that world – of shadows and startling contrasts, of men and women who are driven to act from basic passions, from greed, hatred, lust, who do not think first, who are not intellectual. And if our fears and terrors are abstract and global – the death of the future, the nuclear winter, famine and war which are still elsewhere yet press in on the suburbs of our consciousness – it is a relief to enter into a world in which emotions and dangers are concrete and immediate. Because we see ourselves self-consciously as intellectuals, a deracinated 'petty bourgeoisie', a dislocated lower middle class, it is pleasurable to enter into the acting out of gut-level transgressions against those codes of respectability and moral dreariness with which the *film noir* is at war. This is the aesthetic equivalent of anarchism: the rebellion of a group that rejects forever the positive, the worthy vision of feasible socialism.

Oh, we would much rather venture down those mean streets, where nihilism reigns supreme.

15

How Much is it Worth?

'After seeing Douglas Sirk's films I am more convinced than ever that love is the best, the most insidious, most effective instrument of social repression.'

Rainer Werner Fassbinder

This piece was written in 1975, and published in the women's liberation journal *Red Rag*. In writing a critique of these two films I was trying to make sense of a desperately unhappy love affair, an experience of reluctant and compulsive desire that had ended in rejection, an experience for which the women's movement – or even the wider culture of the period – had no language. The popular view of being in love as a psychic thunderbolt, a random event, was not very helpful, nor were the moralistic analyses of the women's movement in which jealousy, pain and unrequited love were essentially forms of false consciousness. Even psychoanalysis pathologized, for Freud likened love to a neurotic symptom, or else, like any other romantic, returned it to the dark void of the inexplicable.

Each of these films I saw with other, transient, lovers whose failure to staunch the gaping wound made them less real to me than the figures on the screen, who, like me, fed their pain with operatic arias and obsessive introspection. Fassbinder, especially, became wonderful to me, and I went to considerable lengths to see as many of his other films as possible – not easy, as they were only beginning to be shown in Britain then – until I became disillusioned with what Richard Dyer has called his 'leftwing melancholy', which he defines as 'a view of life that recognises the exploitativeness of capitalist society, but is unable to see any means by which a fundamental change in this society can take place'.[1] There is an emphasis on victims and a sense of entrapment; the characters are marginal in social terms, and there is no inkling of a class acting for itself, no resistance, only suffering. Richard Dyer also contrasts my own enthusiasm for *Petra Von Kant* with Caroline Sheldon's criticisms in an article in which she relegated it to 'the freak show genre of men's films about lesbians'.[2]

It must have been the sense of entrapment that I responded to – here on the screen was a moving, yet aestheticized representation of what I was going through. This same bleak sense of suffering is found in some of Fassbinder's later films, especially *Veronica Voss*, which is shot in black and white. In this film the pain of existence freezes on the screen in jagged images of addiction and the sadistic giving and withholding of that which is most desired. In this film, and I think in *Petra Von Kant*, Fassbinder is clearly identified with his women characters, and I don't think that Caroline Sheldon's accusation of misogyny can be sustained.

I remember that at the *Red Rag* collective meeting at which the article was discussed, one woman said it was very 'economistic'. The emphasis on the cash nexus of love, however, was in the films themselves rather than being an interpretation I imposed on them. An aria from *La Traviata* underlines Petra Von Kant's love; and this opera of Giuseppe Verdi is also about the relationship of erotic love to money: Violetta the courtesan renounces her love for Alfredo, because his sister must marry a man who is a good match, and who would be frightened off by the scandal of Alfredo living with a woman of the *demi-monde*.

Even in relationships not directly constrained by the economic, money can figure as a metaphor for power; that power so hard to locate, to acknowledge in relationships supposedly 'free'.

Jack Hazan's *A Bigger Splash* and Fassbinder's *The Bitter Tears of Petra Von Kant* are both built round a homosexual love affair: in the German film it is a lesbian relationship, in Hazan's a relationship between two men. In each relationship there is an element of inequality, but in each the older, more powerful and successful partner suffers and is abandoned. Both these rejected lovers are also artists: one is a real-life painter, David Hockney, the other, Petra von Kant, an imaginary dress designer. This suggests a preoccupation with the style in which relationships are mediated and roles taken up. Both films depict not just a privileged lifestyle, but one dependent on Taste and Style over and above mere wealth. Both films examine not mainstream bourgeois lifestyles, but the decadent edge where style becomes the ultimate possession.

Jack Hazan's film is a film about Hockney's paintings as well as about Hockney himself. Hockney's paintings are all about surfaces and appearances. The film faithfully reproduces both the paintings and the atmosphere of the paintings – the eerie stillness of objects, the withdrawn silences of human subjects. The film, highly enjoyable as a visual exploration of Hockney's work, is also an exploration of a group of friends, artists and designers – 'little fashion freaks', whose main preoccupation appears to be with style. They move through the watery shadows of their carefully wrought interiors like exotic fish in a tank. Even moods are seen in stylistic terms: when Celia Birtwell is discussing Hockney's depression with his ex-lover, Peter Schlesinger, what she actually talks about is Hockney's flat – it is because of his living-room, Hockney feels, that his friends won't go round to see him: 'He'll have to get rid of the drapes; it looks like a waiting room.' You feel the ennui of an unsatisfactory sexual encounter in New York, not because Hockney and his partner are shown lying apart on a bed, exchanging inanities about what countries they prefer and unable actually to hear each other, but because the sequence opens with a dead, silent, flat shot of the back of a New York apartment block, its monotony repeated in the equally monotonous conversation on the soundtrack.

107

Or again, Hockney wanders blankly through his flat and takes a shower. When he turns on the water, which sprays from all angles of the blue-tiled walls, and submits himself to it, his whole appearance changes; with his hair plastered to his skull and his face screwed up he presents an image of extreme agony. At once the scene changes to a California swimming pool and Peter Schlesinger cavorting with three other young men, this standard image of gay male sexuality an effective contrast to Hockney beneath the lash of the spray, locked in his own sexual longing. The sequence ends with the last of the water swirling down the drain in the now empty shower, a visual statement about an imprisoned sexuality, a hopeless infatuation. Hockney is hermetically sealed in the shower while out there in the Californian sunshine flaunts *his* sexual being – it has relocated itself in the loved person; he is completely cut off from it. This suggests one aspect, although maybe not the aspect Fassbinder had in mind, of the 'repressive' nature of sexual 'love'.

Just as objects signify moods, people become things. Near the beginning of the film we are introduced to Mo seated at a table on which stands a vase of tulips, the plate from which he has eaten, an ashtray. It is a still life and Mo achieves the same level of reality as the ashtray and the vase. Peter Schlesinger, too, is represented as an object – a sex object. We briefly see *his* paintings, but he remains essentially a silent, physical being. We see him making love; we see him dancing hypnotically by himself. In one of the California sequences he climbs from the swimming pool and wanders towards the house where the hostess, herself startled, silent and shy as an animal, displays a collection of stuffed animals. She and the naked young man gaze at each other, wordlessly, and, with his hair plastered back with water, Schlesinger looks as much like a deer as the stuffed heads. He hardly speaks throughout the film, his personality remains opaque, whereas Hockney we can understand because he talks.

As well as being a sex object, Schlesinger is an aesthetic object, to be painted by his lover. Posing mutely, passively,

108

obediently in the early morning sunlight of Kensington Gardens he is again reduced to the status of object.

Some critics have objected to this film and to *Petra Von Kant* because both depict homosexual relationships in a pessimistic light, thus pandering to the conventional view of homosexual love as inevitably unhappy. Yet Hazan's film at least is a realistic description of the way homosexual relationships sometimes *are*; it is merely moralistic to say he ought to have shown *only* happy homosexuality in a 'right on' way.

In any case neither of these films is simply about homosexuality. Both are about sexual relationships in a particular kind of society. In the Hockney film directly, in *Petra Von Kant* symbolically, our society is shown as one in which the cult of possessions vitiates human relationships, reaching an hysterical extreme. Inevitably, personal relationships become ritualized, sex is sexist. Had the subject of the Hockney film been a heterosexual relationship audiences might well have found it exaggerated, a caricature. The power imbalances and 'failure to connect' in love between members of the same sex turns a spotlight on *all* relationships. In these stylized films about stylized people, where artificiality reaches a pitch of aesthetic perfection, there can be a more direct exploration of the way in which economic relations and fetishized social forms structure 'love'. Marriage seems so 'normal' that it is hard to perceive it as constructed, as economic; scrutiny of a relationship that is *not* taken for granted reveals the thwarted nature of *all* relationships more clearly.

Definitions of maleness and femininity also pervade even relationships between members of the same sex. Sex roles have little to do with biology; they are reinforced by economics. The male role equates with money, fame, power and status. Hockney has all these things, therefore he is a man. It's all quite simple. You see him talking to Henry, the New York art dealer, while Henry wallows in the bath. The bathroom is all light, colour, luxury. Hockney is telling stories about his dad. Then the camera momentarily shifts to a darkened bedroom: a boy lies there, his genitals covered now, lying waiting, bored, silent, perhaps resentful, in the harem twilight that condemns him to female status. A second time you return to the bathroom; a second time you are back in the darkened bedroom; but this, you realize, is a different bedroom and it is a different boy lying there. So the two boys, the two sex objects do not even speak to each other, they are locked in feminine isolation while their menfolk flaunt and preen.

And yet it is not so simple. Hockney is the jilted lover. It is he who is depressed, deserted. Love, then, is constructed either as a commoditized exchange, or as an unassuaged longing; the Californian swimming pool is a utopia from which Hockney is forever excluded.

Nor is the objectification confined to sexual relationships. That between Hockney and Kasmin, his dealer, also turns on the cash nexus. Kasmin, desperate at not getting the paintings upon which his own livelihood depends, patiently harangues the artist, begging him for more work. The image of Hockney, round-shouldered, silent, reminds us that he too is valued only for what he can produce. 'I think I'll go now,' is all he says – and repeatedly flight, to New York, is offered as the only alternative to this claustrophobic world and its obsessions with pleasure and beauty. The film is an exposition of the aridity of hedonism; an air of exhaustion pervades the atmosphere of unrelenting style. It's so important to be 'cool'.

The flatness of the emotional atmosphere sucks everyone in. The husband and wife relationship between Celia Birtwell and Ossie Clark seems circumspect to the point of non-existence. Celia Birtwell's place in her circle of friends, as the confidante of male homosexuals, further distances the emotions. The subjects of Hockney's paintings are in the film posed next to the portraits of themselves – which is more real, the painting or the human being? And the only time violence threatens to break out is in relation to painting. Hockney, for no apparent reason, examines his portrait of Patrick Proctor (another painter) at close range with a flaming cigarette lighter. Is he going to set light to it? Later, to the heartrending chords of 'Nessun dorma' Hockney advances on his painting of Schlesinger and slashes the canvas from top to bottom, this act representing

110

(according to the artist himself) not the murder of the lover but dissatisfaction with the work. This is a moment of liberation when Hockney appears to escape, through work, from his habitual repressed passivity.

Why is this moment accompanied by the romantic outpourings, the unrestrained romanticism of Puccini's famous aria? In *The Bitter Tears of Petra Von Kant* a similar moment of unrestraint is accompanied by an equally famous aria from *La Traviata*. Classical nineteenth-century opera is the most eloquent of all expressions of bourgeois love, sexual passion romanticized into *the* great experience, more important than life itself (and often operatically entwined with death). Opera expresses romanticism at a naive, almost unreflecting, unselfconscious level. The relationships explored in these films, on the other hand, have moved away from such transparent acceptance of the romantic. Yet the ironic distance they at times place between 'love' and its protagonists, 'love' and the audience, does nothing to explain; it only expresses a frozen acknowledgement of the stunning horror, the sense of being caught in a vacuum beneath a dome of glass.

Fassbinder's film is remarkably artificial. In the German the dialogue is in classical Alexandrine verse. The film takes place within a single interior: Petra von Kant's apartment. It is divided off like any opera into acts. Costumes and setting are stylized. When Petra von Kant wakes in the morning she wears no make-up, her hair is greasy and flat, pinned scrawnily against her head. But from the start her manner is artificial. Artificial the hectoring, spoilt voice with which she gives orders to her maid; artificial the sugary sweetness with which she agrees to lend her mother money as they chat over the phone; dishonest the pretended charm of a letter she dictates in order to avoid payment of a bill. From the beginning money is there at the centre of these acts and relationships. The silent, martyred maid, her mistress's slave, is paid to service her employer, and her worship of her is therefore at some level offensive – degraded and self-indulgent.

Artificiality is explored in another way when Petra begins her toilette by clasping herself into an elaborate fringed robe and putting on a curly wig. Her cousin Sidonie arrives, equally beautifully bewigged, and dressed in bizarre 1920s clothes.

The two then engage in a strangely naked dialogue about the marriage relationship and how women relate to men. As is often the case, the words are even more powerful than visual images. Sidonie pities Petra for the failure of her marriage; Petra's attempt to explain her experience in a different way is repeatedly negated by Sidonie's insistence on her own interpretation. She only wants to pity Petra. Then, to Petra's brutal account of the disintegration of a relationship Sidonie counterpoints the conventional wisdom of how a woman should be to a man – defer to him in little things, let him feel he's the boss – as Petra relates how her love was eroded by her husband's inability to cope with her growing success as a designer. As she exults in her new freedom, insists on how much she's learnt, Sidonie bewails her misfortune. The climax of this dialogue comes when Petra describes with disgust the way her husband tried to assert his power over her sexually: 'He served me like a bull serves a cow.' Against this she sets her aspirations towards a new humility in relationships.

And all the while Petra von Kant holds a mirror and is making-up her face to artificial, artistic perfection, so that by the end of the sequence she has transformed herself from a sallow, tired woman into a mask of beauty.

The hollowness of Petra's aspirations towards humility are revealed when she forms a relationship with a young woman of working-class origins, Karin Thimm. Against a huge baroque painting, with a nude man prominent in the foreground, which covers one whole wall, with Karin Wagnerian in brass breastplates, Petra literally tied up in a semi-Byzantine creation, Petra's declaration of love is made and Karin reveals the truth about her sordid background – her father a murderer who killed his wife and then himself (a theme repeated in other Fassbinder films).

Petra indulges in grandiose dreams of making Karin a successful model, in helping her, caring for her, inventing and creating her. For, like Peter Schlesinger, Karin is both an obsessively loved object, and somehow the creation of her lover/artist. But the combination is again doomed to failure, and again there is the irony of the powerful, successful and dominating lover condemned by her own success to remain unloved.

Individuals imprison each other in the constructs of the personal relationships they create. But, unlike David Hockney, Petra von Kant gives full rein to the hysteria of despair at being thwarted in love, and in her violent oscillations from hatred to longing and back again we are forced to confront the unreality of such feelings, or rather their unrelatedness to their object. They have more to do with Petra's inner conflicts than with Karin, who is clearly ordinary enough.

Petra confronts her mother and her daughter with her misery and despair. It is then – as she stamps an expensive tea set into the luxurious fur rug – 'What I paid for, that I can break' – that money seems to be revealed as the basis for everything. 'It's money that counts.' Karin demands money when she leaves Petra; an overriding need. Petra's relationship with her mother is also, as she screams, based on the prostitution of having to keep her. Her relationship with her daughter is that she pays for an expensive boarding school in order to avoid having to live with her. Throughout the film Fassbinder reduces the psychological constructs of relationships to the economic realities upon which they are based.

Karin Thimm is presented as a straightforwardly sensual being – like Peter Schlesinger. But is is not so straightforward. When she goes out and gets a man for the night she both denies the importance of the encounter and yet uses it cruelly against Petra. In so far as she rejects the status of thing to which Petra would reduce her she is forced to torture Petra. Yet she is equally tainted by the relationship, has no compunction in using Petra, is egocentrically seeking her own 'place in the sun'. Sexual feeling is just another form of exploitation, another weapon. The man she picks up for the night – 'a big black man with a big black prick' – is likewise degraded by being reduced in racist fashion to another sex object. Petra can only sob, her hands clasping the rails of the bed, as she tries to grapple with the merciless reality of her pain – why does it hurt so much? Isn't it senseless? But it isn't – if it's part of an exploitative pattern found in all relationships.

This film is less about lesbianism than about women's place in society. All the characters are women, but seen through and defined by their relationships with men. The men pressing in on the periphery of the film (though hardly seen) – the black lover, Karin's husband, her brutal father, Petra's brutal husband, the businessmen who are ready to exploit her talent as they will also exploit Karin's: these men do define women and herd them into ghettoes of artificiality. Hysteria flowers within its confines, as it also flowers in the gay ghetto. And no solution is offered. At the end of the film the maid rejects Petra's offer of a new, equal relationship, defiantly packs her bag and leaves to the mocking strains of 'The Great Pretender'. This ambiguous ending presumably suggests the impossibility of new forms of relationship when the old social conditions remain.

Fassbinder is not making the mistake – made by some feminists – of supposing that by some effect of will we can here and now transcend our circumstances and have miraculously unalienated erotic relationships, jettisoning the 'bad' feelings and retaining only the good. He does suggest that obsessions with hopeless love, with relationships that will not work, divert energy that might be put to better use, divert attention from our social situation. He also suggests that hysterical obsessions may represent an escape from the responsibilities of relationships such as that of Petra von Kant with her daughter and her mother.

These films – especially Fassbinder's – are not just about unrequited love, infatuation, rejection, possessiveness and jealousy, or even, ultimately, about homosexuality. They explore the irresponsibility of relationships based on economic exploitation, the frigid consumerism of 'liberated' relationships. And, although it may seem that in these films homosexuality is accepted and acceptable, that is not really the case, for it is accepted only as another object of curiosity, the newest bizarre, exotic thing, to be placed on the table alongside Mo and his tulips, ugliness aestheticized. Genuine longings are twisted into perverse yet picturesque shapes and forms. Yet Petra's desire is in itself valid. That is what makes the agony of her disappointment so painful.

It seems to me now that the insistence on the exploitativeness of a society in which commoditization invades everything is an attempt to grasp the experience of what Fredric Jameson describes as not so much the reduction of culture to the economic, as the explosive expansion of culture to 'the point at which everything in our social life – from economic value and state power practices and to the very structure of the psyche itself – can be said to have become "cultural" in some original and as yet untheorised sense'.[4] It seems to me also that my insistence on the economic is a wish to find *some* explanation (and one that the films themselves are implicit in) for this particular form of unhappiness. Yet the entrapment of the films is that they aestheticize the pain the protagonists seek to escape. A postmodern dilemma – set out, rather than 'explored' in a postmodern way.

16

Death City

Brian de Palma's *Dressed to Kill* was a film singled out by feminists as particularly offensive to women. It was picketed in London; in Bradford paint was thrown at the screen during a performance. Had this not been the case I should certainly never have gone to see it, since I hate violence on film. But I was curious to know what made this film *worse* than all the others. Added to which, I'd seen an earlier de Palma film, *Obsession*, and this was admired by some feminists (not the same ones who picketed *Dressed to Kill*) for its exploration of the Oedipal conflict, and so was open to psychoanalytic analysis. How could a director's work appear as an object of fascination to one group of feminists, an object of loathing to another? Did this indicate the confused and divided state of feminism? Did it on the other hand merely prove the thesis that an 'author' (in this case a film director) is a fiction and that there is no necessary connection between one work and another by the same person?

I sat with a friend in an almost empty Dutch cinema, and awaited the ordeal. About a dozen seats were filled; some men – and women – on their own, a few couples, and three noisy youths who left halfway through. We had dared ourselves to go – perhaps our determination had something to do with our changing relationship to feminism: a distancing from it, or a sense of *it* distancing itself from us. We belonged neither to the psychoanalytic feminists nor to the anti-porn feminists, after all, felt marginalized ourselves in a movement of the marginalized. The auditorium darkened and the film began.

As it opens we watch Angie Dickinson sensuously taking a shower: soft-focus images of a naked woman's body, this could certainly be judged as a fairly routine presentation of woman as sex object, as object of voyeuristic attention. A man enters the bathroom, and when he picks up a razor you think for a moment that he may be going to kill or mutilate her (I imagine that any shower scene in a film has a built-in cultural reference to Hitchcock's *Psycho*). In fact he caresses her; but soon afterwards when they are in bed, it is made clear to the audience that this man is an unsatisfactory lover – the camera stares flatly down at the man pressed on top of Angie Dickinson, who stares upward hopelessly, waiting for the 'wham, bam, thankyou ma'am' to be over.

Later, dressed with curiously old-fashioned formality – looking like a woman out of the early sixties in her matching dress and coat, gloves and bouffant hair – she goes to her appointment with her therapist to lay her problems out before him. He offers tea and sympathy as we learn that her first husband, father of her sixteen-year-old son, went missing in Vietnam; and that her dismal second marriage is driving her to seek satisfaction elsewhere.

After she leaves her therapist she visits the Metropolitan Museum of Art. (I was later told that New Yorkers really do treat art galleries as pick-up grounds.) She wanders from room to room and we become increasingly disorientated, glimpsing corners of rooms, paintings half observed through her eyes or the eyes of someone who is invisibly following her, as the camera circles ever more giddyingly through the galleries, the pictures a threatening phantasmagoria, meaningless, disturbing.

She has met someone, and takes a cab with him downtown. As the cab moves off we see a hand stretch out to pick up the white glove she has dropped. So we know that someone else is also following her. But just as we did not see the man she met, so we do not see this other stranger either.

In the cab the anonymous lover lingeringly removes Angie Dickinson's pristine silken panties and performs oral sex on her until she shrieks with pleasure. The cab driver remains impassive throughout this scene, which feminists found particularly offensive, a form of sex as humiliation.

The cab drives through the grey Manhattan streets, stops in front of an anonymous apartment block and the couple disappears within.

Later Angie Dickinson wakes. Her lover is still sleeping. She gets dressed quietly, not wanting to wake him, and then seats herself at his desk to write him a tender note. Before she has finished she needs something, an envelope perhaps, and opens the desk drawer where, however, instead of an envelope she discovers a medical card from which it is plain that the man with whom she has just slept has VD.

The note abandoned, she becomes desperately anxious to get out of the flat. It is not until she is in the lift that she realizes that in her haste she has left her diamond solitaire behind. Under the deadpan scrutiny of a small girl ('It's rude to stare,' says the child's mother) Angie Dickinson panics. She has to go back, yet she is becoming more and more afraid.

And, on her second trip down in the lift her seemingly partly irrational sense of panic is justified, for she is stabbed repeatedly and horribly to death by a crazed blonde female figure. Blood covers Angie Dickinson's white coat and dress as she is stabbed again and again, the scene reflected in the security mirror, until finally she collapses, a blood-boltered mess, trapped in the lift door.

Out of another flat comes a young and beautiful call girl, who has just spent the afternoon with a customer. It is she who finds the body, and makes screaming for the stairs. From this point, a third of the way into the film, this second woman becomes the heroine, and becomes also the 'detective' who will solve the riddle of the sadistic murder. This is one of the splits in the film.

In her odyssey through New York, pursuing and pursued, this hooker repeatedly finds herself in danger in the streets. For example she meets an apparently threatening group of black youths in the subway; she thinks she is being followed by the murderer, but it turns out to be an incognito woman cop sent to shadow and thus protect her. The film therefore reproduces the stereotypical picture of New York as the dangerous metropolis. It is a city of encounters between strangers, a city of indifference, where no one is safe. It is a civilization that is almost completely commodified: you pay for sex, and you pay for the friendship of your therapist.

Particularly dangerous is the unanchored sexuality of the individuals who fleetingly embrace and then as quickly part. The call girl's customers are not in fact dangerous, on the contrary her professional encounters are displayed in an unmenacing and even enjoyable light, yet there is another side to that as well. By now she has made friends with the murdered woman's son, and we watch her totting up her earnings in her luxurious apartment as she explains her financial motive very clearly to the youth.

As she makes herself up for her evening's 'work', her television screen displays an interview with a transexual; the big screen splits to juxtapose the hooker making-up her face and the man with the mask and hairstyle of a woman describing his life as a woman hidden in a man's body. Another split – however these references to the construction of gender, to the artifice involved in the construction of (feminine) identity, and to the inconsistency between the ideal of sexuality as a source of pleasure and the economic motive of the professional lover, are not really followed up in the film. The director points to the 'problems', but they are simply laid on the table, there are no explorations, and certainly no resolutions.

Well before the end of the film the audience has been made aware that the murderer is a transvestite (or transexual), and that the transvestite is in fact the therapist of the murdered woman. It is easy to guess that the therapist might play some sinister role, since he is played by a big star, Michael Caine, and yet is clearly not the *hero* of the film – which, indeed, has no hero. But even apart from that 'external' signal, we are shown the therapist's split personality becoming increasingly unstuck, so that the dénouement, when the hooker tricks him into betraying himself by performing a dangerous and titillating striptease in his consulting room, comes as no surprise.

For feminists this scene was another of the exploitative passages in the film, but their most profound objection was to the way in which women in the film were shown as victims who were punished for seeking sexual pleasure. What I found in the film was something more complex. The sexuality of both women – the double heroine (the good woman and the bad, wife and whore) – is after all shown as healthy or at least honest. It is the men they encounter who have the problems. Angie Dickinson's first husband was lost in Vietnam (symbolically the graveyard of American potency?); her second is a hopeless lover; the man she picks up is diseased; her therapist is a crazy murderer. The hooker fares little better, for the policeman in charge of the murder case is unhelpful, and is a stereotypical macho guy who gets nervous about the least deviation from male/female norms; her lover (pimp?) deserts her; her only real friend is the murdered woman's son.

His main interest in life is ham radio, and he picks up and listens in on other people's conversations. In a curious scene near the end of the film, after Michael Caine has been arrested and returned to Bellevue Hospital, the boy and the hooker meet in a smart tearoom and over the coffee cups she describes to him in great detail how 'the' operation is performed on a transexual. Although the description is entirely verbal, this scene is quite hard to take with its relentless dwelling on every detail of the procedure. At the end of the recital the boy, open mouthed, merely comments: 'Me, I think I'll stick to electronics.' In other words the only decent male figure in the film, an adolescent, is positioned as asexual.

So, if the film is exploitative in its treatment of women, in this it reflects an exploitative world of commoditized sex, and it also paints an unrelentingly negative picture of *male* sexuality. It is the female characters who appear sympathetic, albeit endangered. Transvestism and transexuality are, as must now be evident, extremely negatively viewed – equated with murderous insanity. To meddle with gender, it is implied, is just too dangerous, too mutilating. We are stuck in a world in which women's search for sexual fulfilment is doomed because men are so awful.

In an eerie coda to the film the transvestite, now clad in a nurse's uniform, overpowers his keepers and escapes from the ward full of ghostly mental patients to track down the hooker. She has taken refuge with the adolescent boy in a child-like sibling relationship. The escape and final confrontation, terrifying as they are, turn out to be a nightmare, and at the end the hooker is left cuddling the boy.

Whether feminists were right or wrong to argue that *Dressed to Kill* should not be screened – and their choice does seem rather arbitrary given that there is such a wealth of repulsive violence on celluloid – their action diverted attention from the film's total content, which, although perhaps meretricious, was more interesting than they were willing to acknowledge. The word 'postmodern' was not in common usage in 1980, when the film was made, but today we might see this as a very postmodern work. It is postmodern, for example, in its flat and almost unemotional display of insoluble problems which are not explored, but merely gestured at in a take it or leave it way. The characters are depersonalized, and the significant emotions of the movie are the primitive ('schizophrenic') ones of horror and excitement. The film is never sad, never joyful, never tragic or optimistic. It is as if the shock of modernity, the shock of New York, has left everyone stunned, deadened and one-dimensional. This is the city of our nightmare, and yet it is the city of pleasure and of dreams as well; the one presupposes the other in a hellish circle from which there is no exit.

Dressed to Kill is a film in which the *family* disintegrates. This was also a silent theme of another – underrated – film made at that time: *Gloria*, directed by John Cassavetes. In *Gloria*, too, the protagonist is a woman in flight from a pervasive menace in the city, always moving on, always travelling through the city. In this film too there is no family – apart from *the* family, the Mafia – and yet the only sane relationship Gloria can have is a pseudo-familial one with a little boy, in which Gloria is both a mother and another child, as they are hunted down to death in Paranoid City. And then at the end they seem to reappear, alive and reunited in a Detroit graveyard. So this is also the death of the urban industrial America with which we are familiar.

These films are very different from *Klute*, made in 1972. The story of *Klute* is similar: a hooker, Bree, becomes the intended victim of a perverted killer. She too is alone, independent yet (for that very reason) menaced in New York City. Christine Gledhill and other feminist film critics[1] have discussed *Klute* as a contemporary example of *film noir*, yet it is even more conservative: the 'solution' to Bree's 'neurotic' lifestyle as a sort of liberated hippy is that she is saved by the silent, pure detective (after whom the film is named, significantly), and he returns her to patriarchy in its natural rural setting – marries her and takes her off to the country. But by 1980 even this nostalgic solution has been abandoned; indeed in *Dressed to Kill* it is the therapist – that is, the man in the patriarchal role of authority – who is the most dangerous of all.

In *Gloria* and *Dressed to Kill* women are at last truly alone in the city, and that city is the city of death.

17

Not a Testimony

The commodification of contemporary life always made an exception of the Soviet Union. The construction of the USSR as the Other of Western freedom consigned that country to a limbo of non-consumption, behind which lurked the hell of the labour camp, hideous apotheosis of the commodity-less society. Soviet life is described as 'drab', 'dreary', Moscow as a perpetual London wartime.

It is for that very reason that I have always wanted to visit Russia – to perform the miracle of returning to the past, to my earliest memories. I never wanted to go to those resorts on the Black Sea, which look exactly like the Costa Brava; I longed for little Baltic seaside towns which haven't changed for fifty years. And to visit Budapest *was* to return to a slightly less distant period: the 1950s. The intellectuals lounging, disgruntled, in the baroque cafés looked like Oxford undergraduates of the fifties used to look in the less grandiose surroundings of the Kardomah café on Broad Street, while the goods in the crowded shops had just about reached the level of 1955 affluence. Unfortunately a few posters for nude cabaret acts, and some prostitutes in mini skirts suggested that the Hungarians might be about to embark on 'their' sixties.

But for several years now the theoretical journal of the British Communist Party, *Marxism Today,* has pioneered the sale of t-shirts and coffee mugs printed with Soviet motifs. As it has been at the same time engaged in a wholesale deconstruction of the Communist/Marxist project, this must surely have been an intentional irony. Heroic, modernist Soviet agitational design of the 1920s is recycled as a style. A whiff of revolutionary flavour is on sale for desk-bound Londoners, for whom the struggles of the 1920s are distant enough to be 'pure'.

These saleable objects, similar as they are to mugs and t-shirts sold in aid of actual ongoing struggles in countries such as Nicaragua and Chile, thus promote an illusion of support for the real struggle of the Russian people, long after the event. Or perhaps it is a sentimental feeling of support for their contemporary struggle *against* the 'Soviet system'. Or perhaps it goes further than that, perhaps the irony enters the soul of the purchaser as the t-shirt, worn as a smart badge of generalized dissidence, makes its own cynical comment on the evanescence of belief, the illusory nature of radical fervour.

Maybe the popularity of the Soviet composer Dmitri Shostakovich in 1987 is related to this curious reappropriation of an alien past. It may be coincidental that 1987 saw both a new, highly-praised production of his opera *The Lady Macbeth of the Mtsensk District* by the English National Opera Company at the Coliseum in London, and a new prizewinning film, *Testimony,* directed by Tony Palmer, about the composer's life, given its first British screening at the London Film Festival. Tony Palmer said in a talk he gave at the film festival that he had wanted to make a documentary about Shostakovitch for some time – he had already made several films about composers, the fictional *Wagner* and a documentary about Stravinsky, for example – but it would not be far-fetched to discern a trend, for there was also a BBC television series on the composer's life and work.

At first Shostakovich seems an unlikely candidate for appropriation by the West, since, unlike many Soviet artists and intellectuals in the 1930s and 1940s, he avoided martyrdom, and not only survived Stalin and the purges, but gave official support to the government, acquiescing at times both in denunciations of his own works and in attacks on other composers. Yet his twists and turns, his ambiguous accommodations, *could* be seen as a heroic version of the rather less significant intellectual manoeuvres of a section of the British Left intelligentsia, for whom trimming to the prevailing breeze, while hardly a matter of life and death, seems to have become at least a condition of political credibility (to themselves if to no one else). Actually, this comparison trivializes Shostakovich, whose political commitment was rather more profound and who succeeded in condensing in his musical output the deep conflicts and difficulties of twentieth-century revolutionary practice and ideals.

Shostakovich and his music *do* accord with our times, though; the man surviving through the iron years, in the spiritual wasteland of political repression and war, struggling in his music to express the private and public and unravel the connections; the music innovative yet accessible, speaking directly to our feelings, yet ambiguously, with both a triumphalist and a melancholy voice. Consistent with this ambiguity, both *Testimony* and *Lady Macbeth* offer interpretations similar in style and attitude, laying out the ambiguity without comment or exploration, and offering the traditionally Western anti-Stalinist view of the Soviet experience between the wars – but in a new form in which horror is lightened with hysterical playfulness.

The English National Opera Company production of *Lady Macbeth* updates the tale of bourgeois lust and murder to the 1930s. What had originally been a denunciation of life in *pre*-revolutionary Russia, an indictment of loveless bourgeois marriage, of the oppression of women under the old patriarchal regime, and of the horrors of the Tsarist labour camps, becomes instead an attack on the Soviet police state. Such an interpretation might seem to justify itself by invoking Stalin's own denunciation of the opera. After having initially played throughout the Soviet Union with great success, it was panned in *Pravda* as decadent, and was then suppressed until the 1960s. For, in January 1936, Stalin had attended a performance and its explicit sexuality and musical modernism had offended him. Shostakovich later revised the work, toning down its aggressive sexuality.

The current production is of the original version, and is a thrilling, strident, overwhelming experience. It opens on a tableau: the red-haired heroine, the 'Lady Macbeth', Katerina Ismailova (played by Josephine Barstow) is seated on a shabby, green-painted chair at the front of the stage; Axinya the maid is posed statue-like and motionless in the centre, in peasant dress; at the back looms Katerina's father-in-law. The set represents his meat-packing premises. Like the Beaubourg in Paris, the steel set with its ladders, walkways and pipes induces a sense of 'the modern', and there is the surreal, brutal touch of blood-stained meat carcases hanging from hooks, strung across the set. The shabby light and dark green kitchen chairs at the front of the stage, in poignant contrast, recall the humble, old-fashioned aspect of peasant-merchant life, which is negated by the clashing stridency of the music and the choruses of the crowd.

Initially the crowd consists of peasant workers at the meat-packing factory, from whom Katerina's separateness makes little sense in terms of a post-revolutionary scenario, unless to suggest the perpetuation of class differences in Soviet society. But the hatred she later inspires appears individual rather than class based, and in any case the guests at her wedding, who express it, are not peasants, but are dressed with provincial smartness, and in addition they themselves become the prisoners in the Siberian labour camp along with Katerina herself.

In the first act, Katerina is clearly oppressed by her threatening father-in-law, Boris, who both tyrannizes over her and lusts after her in the absence of her weak, impotent husband. That Boris happens to be played by a black singer fortuitously adds to a reminiscence of 'modern' American musicals, but like so much else, it does not really matter – or seems not to matter – whether or not this is an intentional effect. Willard White's powerful, limping presence adds to the atmosphere of personal menace; that he happens to be black (and of course, black artists have every right to play 'white' parts, and perhaps this should not even be a matter for comment) does however add to the atmosphere of 'modernness' created by the production as a whole. This is also true of the three silent furies who preside over the action in ultra-fashionable mourning gowns and veils of the late twenties or early thirties. These costumes convey a bleak sense of provincial stuffiness, of the longeurs of life far from Moscow for Katerina, who expresses an aspiration towards an altogether other life. Again this is a critique of bourgeois ways of life that makes little sense translated into the post-revolutionary setting.

Katerina is freed from her ennui by the irruption of a virile worker, Sergei. The peasant woman whose silent figure was so striking at centre stage when the opera opened, warns of his reputation as a seducer, and later there develops a scene of hysterical sexual longing in which she caresses herself frantically and is assaulted by the male workers, who symbolically attack the meat carcases with their knives as the brassy music hammers and bangs at the senses.

Soon Katerina and Sergei engage, and the violence of their lust is expressed both in the cynical music and in the sometimes vulgarly choreographed movements of the singers. From this point the 'tragic' line of the story develops: Katerina announces that, for her at least, this is a relationship of passionate love ('Now I have a real husband'); Boris, maddened by jealousy and frustration, has Sergei savagely flogged. The scene is represented symbolically – the workers paint Sergei's back with slashes of red paint – and indeed throughout the action these male workers are represented as a brutal, mechanical force (they will later reappear costumed in scarlet military uniforms as the state police). But whether the meat-packing enterprise, the meat carcases and the workers like automatons symbolize the timeless brutality of the masses, or of modern life, or of the Soviet version only, is unclear.

Katerina is goaded by the outrage against her lover into murdering her father-in-law; she feeds him salaciously with poisoned mushrooms. The old man's funeral is enacted in Brechtian style with a drunken priest and Katerina herself half naked beneath her long mourning veil; later she induces Sergei to collaborate in the murder of her husband – a macabre garroting, after which the husband's body is strung up on a pulley. She then marries Sergei, but the marriage festivities are like a cartoon by Georg Grosz as

127

the stage is overrun by drunken guests in fashionable print dresses and hats, and, amid scenes of orgiastic, lewd debauchery, Katerina is denounced by a malcontent employee who had discovered her husband's body in the cold store.

These set pieces appear true to the words of Shostakovich himself, who described his work as 'a tragic satirical opera'. 'By satirical,' he explained, 'I do not mean ridiculous or laughable. On the contrary . . . I wanted to create a kind of satire that exposes, unmasks and makes you hate . . .'[1] In the current production, however, the ferocious, jeering atmosphere, although effective, is to some extent cast loose from its own meaning by being updated to the Stalin period. Corruption, the spite of the police chief and exile to Siberia have resonance in Soviet terms, but their relationship to the central drama are no longer clear. A meaningful critique of Soviet family life and the position of women would have had to be different.

Yet because this is a postmodern rather than a modernist staging, the inconsistencies are unimportant – or, at least, are disregarded, set to one side; what matters is that an *impression* is created, a reminiscence or flavour. For example, in the scene in which the police break their way into the wedding ceremony, they break through the 'steel' of the set, revealing that the partitions were made only of paper; there is a vague memory here of frames from an Eisenstein film – the visual signal of figures silhouetted across what now appears as a bridge becomes that of 'political oppression' in the abstract, and is a misuse of echoes of Eisenstein, whose images represented the struggle against and victory *over* a politically repressive regime.

The gloomy and beautiful final act, in which Katerina is cynically betrayed by Sergei, kills the woman who has supplanted her in his affections and dies herself, since she pulls them both into a lake, is the most consistent. The Stalinist connotations are abandoned, and the choruses of the finale hark back more to a sense of 'Russian-ness' than to the 'tragic satire' of which Shostakovich wrote.

The conception of 'tragic satire' is close to what Frederic Jameson described as the blank or unlaughing parody of the postmodern art work. The echoing of styles in the English National Opera staging is just such a postmodern use of pastiche, which Jameson criticizes as a dehistoricizing approach. The satire thus loses its precision and the production is in danger of simply reproducing the standard Western assumptions: that human cruelty, lust, envy, and hatred are unanchored, 'timeless' qualities and that 'Stalin' is simply a code word for 'human evil'.

But perhaps there is also an imprecision in the original work, an uncertainty as to the relationship of sexual passion to its social context. Shostakovich wrote:

I dedicated *Lady Macbeth* to my bride, my future wife, so naturally the opera is about love too, but not only love. It's also about how love could have been if the world weren't full of vile things. It's the vileness that ruins love. ... If conditions had been different, love would have been different too.[2]

A sinister dedication for a bride; but perhaps Shostakovich was alluding here also not to pre-revolutionary Russia but to Soviet life. In the Tsarist context the story – like many nineteenth-century European novels of loveless marriage and murderous adultery – does make sense, but to move the action forward forces us to consider the difficulties that revolutionary socialism has had with the concept of what Engels called 'individual sex love'. It is the very inappropriateness of a bourgeois love story in a post-revolutionary setting that makes even clearer a view of the arbitrariness of love, and a view of love as inevitably spoilt, even as senseless. And this accords with a postmodern sensibility. Eclecticism and pastiche as elements of the postmodern contribute towards a loss of meaning in general; what does this imply in relation to love? There is a sense in which 'falling in love' as an irrational event (a form of neurosis or mental illness, as Freud saw it) may be consistent with the irrationality of the postmodern itself, with the fragmentary, with a meaninglessness in modern life that the postmodern may strive to express. The surrealist view of romantic love as itself fragmentary, incomplete, fleeting and absurd is also consistent with the postmodern – as are, perhaps, other aspects of surrealism.

On the other hand, if nothing is real in the postmodern, if everything is fake, or a joke, a form of street theatre, then love too is a masquerade, an illusion. The only difference is that romanticism both in psychoanalysis and in surrealism contains an aspiration within the illusion, whereas in the postmodern that has gone and we are left with a utopian dream devoid of utopia, a façade that masks a vacuum.

There is a façade-like element in the staging of *Lady Macbeth;* the steel wall of the meat-packing cold store pushes towards us so that events seem to take place at the edge of the stage; even when the bedroom (decorated in traditional Russian style) opens out within the forbidding steel structure, it is only a small and enclosed space; but the steel wall is itself unreal, a paper simulacrum, and it is only in the last act that there is an indistinct sense of the bleak wastes that stretch back beyond the scaffolding of what has now become a prison camp.

Testimony too (which also makes use of the vast, cold steppes to suggest something fundamental about the Russian /Soviet experience) is a masquerade at more than one level. In his National Film Theatre lecture Tony Palmer said that it had not been possible for him to make an actual documentary about the composer's life, because the material is all in the USSR. Consequently the film, shot largely in black and white, has at times the appearance of being a documentary but is a fiction or semi-fiction. It is based on the Shostakovich memoirs, *Testimony,* however, the status of this book is contentious. These memoirs were supposed to 'have been as related to, and edited by, the émigré Soviet musicologist Solomon Volkov'.[3] But Volkov, now resident in New York, and consultant to the film, is regarded as unreliable, even Russians living in the West, such as Mstislav Rostropovich, judging his an 'unbalanced and incomplete' portrait.[4] And, although it is claimed that Shostakovich signed every page of the memoirs' transcript to underwrite their authenticity, these pages have not been produced. The composer's son, Maxim Shostakovich, 'decisively rejected Volkov's claims to authenticity'[5] and, summarizes Christopher Norris, 'one can only regard *Testimony* as yet another phase in the struggle to appropriate Shostakovich's music which has long been waged by ideologues of various colour'.

Nonetheless, the film, like the opera, is an exciting experience in which the onlooker becomes emotionally involved – although, of course, in both cases Shostakovich himself should take a large part of the credit for that. The exaggerated black and white contrasts contrive to resemble silent film in the early sequences, when Ben Kingsley as Shostakovich looks like Buster Keaton – black lips and white face – and seems accidentally to have found himself on the set of a remake of *The Cabinet of Dr Caligari*. The element of pastiche is effective in creating an atmosphere of eerie confusion, although exactly to what purpose is unclear. Fellini-like troupes of circus figures appear through mist, and mill about in an unexplained way.

In other passages, particularly those relating to the Second World War, genuine documentary footage is spliced into the new film, which gives a surreal 'authenticity' to Tony Palmer's frames. The fictional film of Shostakovich on his goodwill tour to the United States accurately recreates the harsh, hysteric feel of newsreels a few crucial years later, in the Cold War period – the newsreels of Alger Hiss, the Rosenbergs, of Whittaker Chambers before the House UnAmerican Activities Committee.

On the other hand it was a mistake to insert passages from Eisenstein – astonishing crowd scenes – which serve only to illustrate the superiority of the Soviet director's mastery of film, while the insertion of footage from both Soviet and Nazi celebration parades is cheap, signalling as it does the dubious cliché that there is only one modernist 'totalitarianism' in which Communism and Nazism are one. Worst of all, verging on the exploitative, is the use of concentration camp footage, heaps of emaciated corpses appearing on the screen simply to give a vague sensation of horror.

Tony Palmer's contempt for the Soviet Union was clear from his NFT talk; his lack of respect for an experience, however flawed and terrible, results in a grandiose project, sometimes thrilling, often bombastic, and one that tells us surprisingly little about Shostakovich and his relationship to the period in which he lived. The drama is interpreted in entirely individual terms: Stalin pitted against Shostakovich, and ambiguous confrontation ('I am the enemy you loved,' says Stalin on his deathbed), which leaves unexplained and indeed unexplored the reasons for the composer's loyalty and commitment to the regime.

A much more interesting and political film could have been made about the astonishing turbulence, confusion and divided loyalties of the first twenty years of the Revolution. Or the director could have explored how much there was in Shostakovich of the eternal survivor – portrayed in central European works such as Brecht's plays, Döblin's *Berlin Alexander Platz* and *The Good Soldier Schweik,* for example; while his life would surely have better lent itself to a comic or satirical rendering, than to the humourless gloom that enwraps most of the film, and Shostakovich would have been more interesting as a disreputable, cynical yet lively survivor than as a romantic hero who spends his time mooning about his drawing-room and strumming at the grand piano in hope of inspiration while the net curtains blow inward through a slightly bleached mist of dry ice.

To portray Stalin *simply* as the evil monster is also not good enough. This individualization of Soviet history depoliticizes, indeed dehistoricizes it. It is as if without the 'accident' of Stalin's personality the Soviet Union would have turned into a decent, Western-style parliamentary democracy. At the end of the film we read on the screen that Shostakovich completed 147 musical works and Stalin killed thirty million people. This is not true. One man cannot kill thirty million people. A political situation arose in which violence and terror became possible, but Stalin was only one element in the situation. Nor did Stalin seek to conquer the whole of Europe, although the film, incorrectly, tells us that this was the reason for the Nazi-Soviet pact. ('With whom can I now conquer Europe?' Stalin yells, on hearing that Hitler has broken the pact by invading Russia.) Stalin's policy, both before and after the Second World War was dictated primarily by well-founded fears as to the intentions of the Western powers. This justifies neither Soviet domination of the socialist bloc, nor the Soviet failure to defend, for example, the Greek partisans. With the tacit acquiescence of Stalin they were destroyed, initially, by the British, who displayed no compunction about interfering in the internal affairs of another country either. But in a perhaps unexpected way the portrayal of Stalin, who sits at his desk not in the Kremlin but in a deserted hangar – a disused corner of Ciné Citta perhaps – amid the ubiquitously swirling dry ice, illustrates the hollow centre of this work. The cliché isn't questioned, but merely reproduced. And the surprise is that this should occur in a film that strives with some success to be visually innovative.

There are unsuccessful passages in which detached or almost abstract imagery appears as an illustration of the music. Then, the film veers dangerously close to a commercial, (although advertising what, we do not know) for it draws on the same combination of classical music and 'artistic' imagery. The way in which ads draw both on visual reminiscence of the 'old masters' and – increasingly – on modernist and surrealist imagery is well known, and *Testimony* may at moments be experienced as vaguely exploitative in the same way. Definitely not realist, either as documentary or as fiction, it is not quite avant garde either, and is emotionally 'easy' when perhaps it should be challenging and questioning.

Yet the pleasure of the film is undeniable. There is pleasure in the pastiche itself, in the stark and sometimes mysterious black and white. This pleasure raises the question of the roots of our delight in the kitsch, the decadent, and (if we consider ourselves to be 'Left wing') in the politically reactionary too. Perhaps it appeals, as soap opera is said to appeal, to a 'tragic structure of life',[6] to a recognition that life does not 'work out', that there are no happy endings, that nothing works, life is fragmentary, our lives do not form a coherent whole, motivation is always occluded. We can twist a perverse beauty out of this very knowledge. Such perversity is said to be part of the urban sensibility too:

How much beauty there is to discover ... enveloped in old age, in sickness, in grief, in severe anguish ... How fine the sick complexions of big-city children are, and see how often their features take on a marvellously severe beauty precisely as a result of need and deprivation. Even depravity and insolence can possess beauty, energy, indeed greatness.[7]

This is an aspect of human response with which socialism has yet to come to terms.

Is our experience, then, of the vitality and energy of the recent production of *Lady Macbeth* and the at times icy beauty of Palmer's *Testimony* a kind of false consciousness? The concept of false consciousness has been largely rejected as élitist, as suggesting that 'we' the 'left', or the 'avant garde' for that matter, are in possession of true consciousness, while it is the masses, or the consumers of popular culture whose consciousness is false, faulty. But what of our own 'false consciousness'? If we believe in an unconscious, in hidden motives, in bad faith, even just in mistakes, and certainly if we believe in the irrational, must we not concede that our beliefs, and those of others, might be wrong?

Alternatively, our experience of the music of Shostakovich – tragic *and* hopeful, exuberant *and* heartrending – as filtered through these postmodern interpretations, may serve a more contradictory purpose. Maybe the experience of these art works offers a means whereby we can subjectively reconcile our immense cynicism towards the Soviet experience with our aspirations to a form of life and a society different from our own, while at the same time we cling to our scepticism.

Also, in both *Testimony* and *Lady Macbeth* a Western audience may experience 'Russian-ness' or 'Soviet-ness' as an exotically frightening sense of horror that is at the same time aestheticized by a pastiche-avant garde series of images, and emotionally experience a form of longing for, or melancholy awareness of, some lost object of desire. The experience is 'postmodern', perhaps because of our knowing awareness, all the time, of these dislocated responses: simultaneously we appreciate the pastiche of

Soviet life; pastiche; and our knowledge that it *is* the flavour of modernism that disrupts the narrative, and for which we are now culturally ready.

Across screen or stage storms the cultural collage that is our life of the senses in the city today. The music of Shostakovich, at once modern and deeply popular, expresses that dislocation, that ambivalence.

18

Love

'We could spend a lovely quiet evening, so quiet that in the end you might even feel it was uncanny.'

Franz Kafka to Felice Bauer

In Prague just before the First World War a man nearing thirty meets a young woman one evening in the apartment of his friend's family. She is on a visit from Berlin. A few weeks later he writes to her, inspired by a discussion they had had concerning a possible visit to Palestine. In the space of a few more weeks this correspondence has become a love affair. The man is Franz Kafka, the woman is called Felice Bauer.

In the absence of further meetings all the uncertainties of a developing passion orientate themselves round the means of communication, the letters themselves. There is the difficulty of finding out Felice's correct address; the anxieties when a letter is delayed, or a delivery mistimed; and the drama of their actual arrival, usually at Kafka's office. The momentous wafers of paper seem almost too fraught with meaning to be desecrated by opening them; the reading of their contents invariably gives rise to further uncertainties, since the difficulty of interpreting the exact nuance of meaning in every word and sentence is so great. Misunderstandings proliferate, yet these developments form the substance of the love that they themselves interrogate, or rather that they themselves actually create. Their development is like that of a novel in letter form; Kafka reconstitutes Felice Bauer's past with the aid of a

136

chronological sequence of photographs she sends him of herself as a child and a girl; in return Kafka describes the eating regimen and daily timetable which enable him to do creative work. Letters are exchanged between the mothers of the pair; and Felice also writes anxiously to Kafka's friend Max Brod. At a later stage, Felice's friend, Grete Bloch, is drawn into the correspondence, to act as mediator. Long after the whole affair is over, Grete Bloch will claim that she had a child by Kafka (it is virtually certain that this is a false claim). She, like Kafka's last love, Milena Jesenska, will die in a concentration camp.

Kafka's letters to Felice Bauer are valued as literature for what they reveal about Kafka, the modernist writer who most clearly reveals our urban angst, our 'modern condition' to us. His intense sensitivity calls everything into question, he cannot bracket off or take for granted what to others would be the hardly noticeable sensations, the trivial details of street life, office life, home life; for him sensation is experienced as always and imminently overwhelming. He comes always fresh to the noise and movement of city life, whereas we have grown used to it. His only response can be 'fear and indifference' – and to write. Writing is for him a substitute both for life and for death:

Believe me, Felice, your assumptions are incorrect. My attitude to my writing and my attitude to people is unchangeable; it is a part of my nature, and not due to temporary circumstances. What I need for my writing is seclusion, not 'like a hermit', that would not be enough, but like the dead. Writing, in this sense, is a sleep deeper than that of death.[1]

He knows that Felice cannot and will never understand his relationship to his writing:

I have no literary interests, but am made of literature, I am nothing else and can be nothing else. The other day I read the following story in a *History of Devil Worship*: 'There was a cleric with a voice so sweet and so beautiful that all who heard it were filled with joy. One day a priest heard the sweetness of these sounds and said: 'This is not the voice of a man, but of the devil.' In the presence of all the many admirers he exorcised the demon and drove him out, whereupon the corpse (for this body had been animated by the devil instead of a soul) disintegrated and stank.' The relationship between me and literature is very similar to that, except that my literature is not as sweet as that monk's voice.[2]

Precisely, however, because Felice does not understand and is incapable of comprehending this sinister relationship, she too is necessary to him, representing the stability he lacks:

Are you aware, and this is the most important thing, of a continuous relationship between yourself and a reassuringly distant, if possible infinite height or depth? He who feels this continuously has no need to roam around like a lost dog, mutely gazing around with imploring eyes; he never need yearn to slip into a grave as if it were a warm sleeping bag and life a cold winter night; and when climbing the stairs to his office he never need imagine that he is careering down the well of the staircase flickering in the uncertain light, twisting from the speeding of his fall.[3]

The Penguin edition of the letters includes a biogrpahical note about Felice Bauer, which emphasizes precisely this stability, her normality. 'All testimonials and reports on Felice Bauer,' the note tells us – rather like a testimonial itself –

emphasize her efficiency and common sense in practical matters – qualities which, as Kafka says, he himself lacked entirely, and which throughout his life he often admired extravagantly in others . . . Felice appears to have been a positive, uncomplicated person. Kafka once described her as 'a happy, healthy, self-confident girl'. She liked pretty clothes, enjoyed travelling, but was prepared to sacrifice much for the sake of helping her family. Her taste in literature, art and furnishing was that of the middle classes of her time. She evidently had little understanding of Kafka's literary work.[4]

We are told that after her relationship with Kafka had ended she married a 'well-to-do Berlin businessman'. With him she eventually emigrated to the United States, where she sold Kafka's letters to a publisher a few years before her death.

We are left wondering why a young bourgeois woman such as this should have reciprocated Kafka's love, or even responded to his letters. No doubt there was something more 'complicated' about her than the patronising biographical note allows. She was engaged to Kafka twice. It must have been important to her. Their relationship dragged on for five years. We may speculate whether she passionately desired the thin, thin young man with his great, dark eyes and child's face, or whether her dominant feeling was the 'compassion' to which Kafka refers. We wonder what she felt when she heard, seven years after their engagement had ended, that he had died of tuberculosis. Did she dream of him forever afterwards, or merely smile occasionally in indulgent reminiscence of a youthful absurdity? What was her life in Berlin as a bourgeois housewife during the Weimar Republic, and afterwards in America (and where in America)? We can imagine her in the publisher's office in 1955 with the letters, as a blue-rinsed, Americanized matron of Eisenhower's America, or as having grown old with central European dignity.

But we do not know. We know so little about her, save what filters through Kafka's 'Kafkaesque' responses to her. There is a gaping hole in the text, an almost total silence where the 'other half' of this romance should be. Cast in the thankless role of his 'lucky star' – his 'muse' as the Penguin blurb predictably puts it – her shadowy existence places her as the silent Other of all romantic love, this Other being the representation of the mystery that romantic love is said to be.

Yes, this emptiness, this absence betrays a truth of romantic passion. And these letters reveal to us the evolution, or perhaps it is the disintegration, of the romantic project in the machine age. Here is the love letter just as it is about to be superseded by the telephone (and oddly enough Felice works for the firm 'Parlograph', who produce a kind of dictaphone, so that she is herself part of the developing modern communications system). Soon, it is true, the telephone will have its own romantic aura:

139

We are like the person in the fairy tale for whom a sorceress, at his express wish, conjures up, in a supernatural light, his ... betrothed in the act of turning over a book, of shedding tears, of gathering flowers, close by the spectator and yet very far away, in the place where she actually is at the moment. We need only, so that the miracle may be accomplished, apply our lips to the magic orifice and invoke ... the Vigilant Virgins to whose voices we listen every day without ever coming to know their faces, and who are our guardian angels in the dizzy realm of darkness whose portals they so jealously guard; ... by whose intervention the absent rise up at our side, without our being permitted to set eyes on them; the Danaïds of the unseen who incessantly empty and fill and transmit to one another the urns of sound; the ironic Furies who, just as we were murmuring a confidence to a loved one, in the hope that no-one could hear us, cry brutally: 'I'm listening!'; the ever-irritable handmaidens of the Mystery ... priestesses of the Invisible, the Young Ladies of the Telephone.[5]

Soon rapid transit as well as electronic communications will make romance possible for those who live far apart – indeed this is already the case for Kafka and Felice – and in the future the international, even the intercontinental love affaire will become commonplace, one means among others of heightening the 'romantic effect'. For, as Freud said:

An obstacle is required in order to heighten libido; and where natural resistances to satisfaction have not been sufficient men have at all times erected conventional ones so as to be able to enjoy love.[6]

In Kafka's letters love is constructed not merely as more difficult on account of the obstacles in its way, but as the impossible. Kafka consistently fantasizes a moment of communion which is death-like in its calm: 'dearest, to lie at your feet and be calm, that would be best'. Kafka refers to this dog-like devotion as shameful or pathetic, yet also as an immense relief, for it manages to approximate love to solitude, of which romantic passion is in fact a variant. What the romantic temperament requires is the love effect in a pure form, if possible undiluted by reality. Just as women are said to read romantic pulp fiction in order to experience this effect in a comparatively harmless way (or even as a form of innoculation against its real-life counterpart) so Kafka in his letters cherishes and cultivates all the emotional responses of romantic passion – as when he creates a crisis out of a letter delayed by a few hours – in the purest form, the form least diluted by that everyday life he found so exhausting and exhaustingly trivial. When reality threatens to enter in, when there is even a possibility that Felice might actually agree to marry him, he panics.

He recognizes that for others the trivia of daily life forms the substance of a love that is different from the romantic, as when he writes to Milena Jesenska:

I did not misunderstand you in regard to your husband. You pour the whole secret of your indestructible holding-together, this rich inexhaustible secret, again and again into the worry over his boots. Something in it torments me, I don't know exactly what. It's after all very simple: should you leave him he will either live with another woman or go and live in a boarding house, and his boots will be better cleaned than now. This is silly and not silly. I don't know what torments me so much in these remarks.[7]

The love that expresses itself in worries about the cleaning of boots is, Kafka implies, a matter of fact, bread-and-butter love, the nourishing love of daily life – different from the agitation and anxiety of his overwrought romantic passion.

Milena Jesenska lived in Vienna, where Freud, of course, practised. Psychoanalysis became an investigation of the basis of erotic passion. In the process the focus moved from love to sexuality; romantic love was revealed as a screen concealing other, stranger desires. In all the great European cities – in Paris, in Berlin, in post-revolutionary Moscow and Leningrad, heterosexual love came under the spotlight, proved to be something else. Radicals looked askance at its signs and symptoms. Yet intensity of feeling was as important as ever. The position of women and the nature of femininity was a part of all this. The part that women were to play in love was changing.

Kafka's love letters are a part of the same romantic project in the 'modern' era as the case histories of Freud, which they resemble, with their false starts, blind alleys and obstinate frustrations. Kafka, the protagonist, is the modern hero (an anti-hero, inevitably) in love; Felice, his beloved, is cast (even if this is in part because we cannot read *her* letters) in the traditional role of Other, a blank onto whom is projected the radiant – or lurid – colours of the lover's psyche.

Nineteenth-century romanticism had always defined love in this way – as essentially a product of the imagination. Stendhal used an elaborate yet telling metaphor for the psychological process whereby love comes into being:

At the salt mines of Salzburg, they throw a leafless wintry bough into one of the abandoned workings. Two or three months later they haul it out covered with a shining deposit of crystals. The smallest twig, no bigger than a [bird's] claw, is studded with a galaxy of scintillating diamonds. The original branch is no longer recognisable.[8]

In other words, the beloved, who triggers the passion of the lover, *disappears* under the accretions of the lover's sentiments, is recreated into something new – and much more remarkable. The woman who is loved is no more than the raw material out of which the lover *creates* her as a love object – a production like the production of a work of art.

In this rendering of love it is the man who loves and the woman who simply acts as inspiration. On the other hand in nineteenth-century opera, perhaps the most intense expression of the romantic view of love, heroines also experience this active romantic passion. In opera, betrayal and death are often substitute forms of consummation. At the best of times, love is absence; in Madam Butterfly's most famous aria, for example, she describes with passionate intensity her reunion with her lover – describes him coming to meet her, he's coming closer, he's climbing the steps – but all the time he *isn't there*, he's a figment of her imagination, raised up by her longing. For romantic love represents longing, represents a desire for something (someone) who stands in for that which was always lost.

Freud's treatment of (largely female) neurosis in the last years of the nineteenth century in Vienna led him to a full-scale investigation of erotic love, and the psychoanalysis he created had the effect of both deconstructing and reintegrating romantic heterosexual love. Psychoanalysis theorizes and practises both within the romantic tradition and against it. On the one hand Freud reduces romantic love to a symptom of neurosis: 'Sexual over-estimation is the origin of the peculiar state of being in love, a state suggestive of a neurotic compulsion.'[9] This is Freud the scientific rationalist. Yet on the other hand the core of the Freudian project is the elevation of the infant's love for the parental figures into the ultimate romantic quest. Romantic love to that extent becomes essentially incestuous (and therefore *always* forbidden). This incestuous love is the lost object of desire around which the identity of each of us is built. The privacy of the bourgeois family home is the stage of an eternal opera of repressed desire. Love is always impossible, yet is built into character and consciousness.

Freud opposed the standards of sexual morality current in his lifetime: 'Sexual morality as society – in its most extreme form, the American one – defines it, seems to be very contemptible. I stand for an incomparably freer sexual life, although I myself have made very little use of such freedom.'[10] This was, however, hedged about with provisos in the classic psychoanalytic writings. Psychoanalysis has always held in tension the aspiration towards fuller sexual enjoyment and the impossibility of a love wholly free of inhibition – an impossibility because of its basis in 'the family romance'.

This makes psychoanalysis in a sense one more utopian, romantic quest. Wilhelm Reich, who, for a time, was a disciple of Freud, diverted Freudian insights in a different direction. An alternative tradition developed: the belief that sexual repression is to be abolished. This would have the effect of destroying romanticism, which became little more than an effect of repression. Reich was another utopian, but his ideal was rationalist utopia. Desire, sex, would be freed from the social. For example, Reich believed that the highest form of orgasm was one unaccompanied by any fantasy. For fantasy is the mental and emotional component, and Reich wished to return the sexual instinct to its biological basis.

These alternative views: the pessimistic, or at least ironic romanticism of Freud, and the optimistic biologism of Reich, have continued to be immensely influential. Attempts were made, before and after the Second World War, to integrate their ideal of a fuller sexual life into a new and more modern ideal of marriage, 'companionate marriage'. This was a middle-class ideal of the 1930s in the English-speaking world, but after World War Two family planning and marriage guidance organizations aimed to extend it throughout society. In a sense companionate marriage – the domestication of the sexual impulse – had always been part of bourgeois marriage; this new form, however, tried to take account of changes in the status of women, for there was a dawning recognition that their sexual needs as well as those of their husbands needed to be taken into consideration.

Since the divorce rate rose steadily (and today the rate of marriage is falling as well, in Britain at least) this attempt to stabilize marriage by containing a fuller sexuality within its confines could be said to have failed, and 'the sixties' has come to be a coded expression for the renewal of an explicit struggle over meanings in the sphere of erotic love. Once again the works of Reich were invoked, and the project was once more conceived of – at first – as the breaking free both from externally imposed codes of behaviour, and from the 'character armour' of inhibition in the interests of spontaneity and fulfilment. Whereas, however, in the 1920s it had been the triumph of heterosexuality over perversion and neurosis that had been the expected outcome, in the 1960s it was to be the emergence of diverse sexualities from the prison house of 'compulsory heterosexuality'.

In the period between the two world wars, many radicals had assumed that a freer sexuality would act as a challenge to the capitalist status quo. Antonio Gramsci, Italian militant and Communist, discusses this in his *Prison Note-books*. There, he refers to the attempts of Henry Ford and other American industrialists to interfere in the private lives of workers, and enforce 'puritanical' standards of behaviour. Yet Gramsci shows himself ambivalent towards the conditions of life that are to be imposed on the 'new worker':

It might seem that in this way the sexual function has been mechanised, but in reality we are dealing with the growth of a new form of sexual union shorn of the bright and dazzling colour of the romantic tinsel typical of the petit bourgeois and the Bohemian layabout. It seems clear that the new industrialism wants monogamy; it wants the man as worker not to squander his nervous energies in the disorderly and stimulating pursuit of ... sexual satisfaction. ... The exaltation of passion cannot be reconciled with the timed movements of productive motions connected with the most perfected automatism.[11]

On the one hand, the 'romantic tinsel' of bourgeois sexuality is decadent, but on the other the new order involves 'repression and coercion'. Gramsci, whose thoughts illustrate the uncertainty of Left as well Right which constitutes part of the general 'sexual crisis' of contemporary life, is aware that there is an incosistency between the libertarian ideology of sections of the bourgeoisie and the scenario of repression outlined above; he is unclear how it can be resolved. He is also aware that the changing role of women is central:

The formation of a new feminine personality is the most important question of an ethical and civil order connected with the sexual question. Until women can attain not only a genuine independence in relation to men but also a new way of conceiving themselves and their role in sexual relations, the sexual question will remain full of unhealthy characteristics.[12]

Yet Gramsci predicted wrongly, in that sexuality itself has been increasingly commoditized in contemporary capitalist society. Both the Right and the Left, and many, though not all feminists, draw back in suspicion from this. For this reason, they draw close together in their opposition to pornography. Truly conservative thought is concerned primarily to restore patriarchal authority. From this standpoint, sex is sinful outside marriage, and in the sexual act itself is implicit the subordination of woman to man. This view tends to seem increasingly perverse in a culture in which there is a knowingness, if not a tolerance, about sexual repression and the vagaries of desire; patriarchal sex comes to have a rather sado-masochistic flavour about it.

The Left and feminism are caught in contradictory ideals of sexual behaviour. In the early seventies, Left-libertarian and feminist writings on sexuality were informed by an implicit Reichianism. It was assumed that romanticism was the ideology of female subordination, and that along with sexual repression in general it should be thrown off. This would make possible the flowering of an essential female sexuality.

Yet there was soon a retreat from the utopianism of Reich. Instead, women undertook an investigation of the difficulties of 'reconstructing' one's desires and one's gendered responses. In this discourse 'sexuality', 'desire' and 'gender' displaced love as the object of interrogation. Very gradually, there was an implicit rehabilitation of romanticism; feminists ceased to denounce romantic pulp fiction and soap operas as vehicles for reactionary ideology, and emphasized instead the pleasure these aspects of popular culture gave to millions of women, themselves included.

Psychoanalysis has been the theoretical tool which feminists have used in order to try to understand why women suffer in love, or connive in their subordination. Women's relationship to their own emotions and to femininity becomes a problem, but it remains a largely psychological, personal problem within a society assumed to be 'patriarchal'.

For the feminists who have attacked pornography, by contrast, there are no psychological problems, there is only male oppression and violence, and pornography serves no purpose but to brutalize and even destroy women. They are aware of pornography as part of the expanding communications industry, but to them that is of less importance than its significance in terms of men: it is just one form of male hatred of women.

Only a few feminists have linked the 'sexual crisis' to the general commoditization of contemporary society, or with the ethical vacuum of the 'postmodern'. And the two are linked. For it is not just the 'dirty' sex of porn, nor just the defiant and transgressive sex of the avant garde that become objects of consumption – whether as hardcore videos or art films. Romantic love is centrally involved. With the waning of both political and religious beliefs in the West, romantic love becomes that which we most truly live by. It is not just 'the family' that is the basic unit of society, it is the romanticized, eroticized family. This family is the underlying justification for the consumer society, which it redeems. The zone of privacy we create (if we can) with mortgages, dream kitchens, and matching bedlinen and wallpaper is a shrine to Freud's 'family romance'. The whole culture is eroticized, including children.

The feminist discourse inaccurately refers all problems back to 'patriarchy'. Like Gramsci, feminists recognize that women must become independent, but this becomes a question of escaping from a patriarchal universe, and so does not deal with the commoditized ethical vaccum in which we are actually living, and which is not the responsibility only of 'men'.

Julia Kristeva is one of the few women theorists to have written explicitly about love. She has made the claim that love, as seen in action in the practice of psychoanalysis, is the secular replacement of religion. She is concerned to demonstrate that psychoanalysis is an 'ethics of love' in the sense that it takes up a committed position, insisting that *truth* is at stake in the practice of the psychoanalytic cure. For there can be no concept of cure without some system of values, a concept of 'health' to underpin it. The analytic process is not just a strange and endless wandering in a strange country, Freud's 'hinterland' of the unconscious; although the postmodern appropriation of psychoanalysis might make it seem that way; there is a goal, to 'get better'.

There is a difference, none the less, from religion. Christianity, and particularly the Roman Catholic Church, of which Julia Kristeva writes, claimed that its truth was for all (as does revolutionary Marxism). The truths, however, that, according to Kristeva, arise in the context of the psychoanalytic cure, and which are given voice through the transference-love relationship which is the core of the treatment, are specific and particular truths, true only for this time and place, this individual, this relationship. In this respect the therapeutic endeavour is a subjective experience which – like romantic passion – often appears utterly mysterious to outsiders. *This* truth *is* relative. And it is, Julia Kristeva tells us, like love: 'When I am in love, there is palpitating, passionate, unique meaning, but only right here and now, a meaning that may be absurd in another conjunction.'[13]

Kristeva equates this state both with transference-love (the love between analyst and patient) and with mother-love. She dwells on love partly in reaction against the feminist and avant garde emphasis on 'desire' that dominated the theory of the 1970s. But her discussion occludes one important characteristic of romantic love, which makes it different from either therapeutic or maternal love: it seeks above all to render the transient permanent; seeks to preserve *itself* at all costs. In this it is utopian. The lover wants to hold onto the intensity of being in love forever. By contrast the mother and the analyst (or at any rate the 'good' mother and the 'good' analyst) desire the independence of the child or patient, and thus, in a sense at least, the 'end' of the relationship.

In offering us a unique love within the therapeutic relationship as a means of replenishing the postmodern world with meaning, Julia Kristeva merely returns us, however, to the liberal individualism of the 1950s. At that period, too, psychoanalysis emphasized the 'uniqueness of the individual' and the consequent inadequcy of political solutions. It was the very failure of this half-truth that led to the sexual questioning of the 1960s and 1970s.

Toril Moi points out that the individual case histories discussed by Julia Kristeva in the context of her views on

psychoanalysis and love, are 'peculiarly postmodern ...
borderline cases',[14] for whom there is neither the forbidden
nor is there love. Here, the postmodern is seen as negative,
as pathological. Julia Kristeva's solution is to reassert the
apolitical ethics of psychoanalysis, yet without acknowl-
edging *its* romanticism. To say that psychoanalysis is the
secular replacement of religion is merely a well-worn
truism, and assigns it an implicitly conservative role.

Yet at least she acknowledges the existence of a 'moral
crisis' to which there has to be an ethical response. For the
Left and for feminism, the problem has always been to
square the ethical with the political. The contemporary
moral and sexual crisis is part of a wider crisis of authority
sometimes referred to as postmodernism, a 'moment in
the history of the West ... pervaded by profound yet little
comprehended change, uncertainty and ambivalence'.[15] So
where is love in the postmodern? Do we simply move
between the contradictions as though they did not exist?
Has love, for us, become *manifestly* a bricolage of inconsistencies, a jumble of worn-out folk wisdoms, psychological
truisms and confused hungers?

For the individual – not necessarily. Many women and
men resolve these problems more or less satisfactorily for
themselves. For Julia Kristeva these individual solutions
are advanced as though they were general solutions. This
they cannot be. Individuals get by; but Western culture is
incapable, it seems, of developing either a coherent view
of love or consistent social practices whereby to regulate
it.

There is a cultural void. The liberal tolerance of Enlight-
enment thought is a passive element within which the
ever-threatened backlash and the spiral of transgressive
aspirations writhe indecisively, and the terrifying apparition of AIDS merely adds to our disorientation in a world
in which hedonism and hell-fire coexist.

To return to the period at which Kafka wrote, to the last
moments of romanticism, romanticism in a modernist
disguise: Proust and Kafka analysed or lived romantic love
as an intensity of unfulfilled or unrequited desire, of which
absence was the key. For them, as for Stendhal, romantic

love was as much an act of the imagination as fiction itself. And, as for Freud, love for them took place in the frenetic modern city with its telephones, its express letters, its trains, its trams, its passages of easy escape for the loved one in flight. Love became a figment of the urban imagination, the urban psyche. Freud's case histories, like the novels and letters of Kafka and Proust, are filled with chance encounters in the street, letters gone astray, assignations in shady regions where the house of ill fame looms in the background, sudden illicit embraces in awkward corners, secrecy above all. In these early twentieth-century cities forbidden love can more readily be lived out, can become real, even as the intensity of desire is displaced onto the lost, the absent, the disappeared: what Baudelaire called 'love at last sight'.

I remember the first night. We lived ... opposite a dress shop, in the door of which a shop-girl used to stand ... we came to an understanding by sign language ... but when I came down in the evening someone else was already there – well this didn't make any difference ... she ... signed to me that I should follow them ... we walked, I following slowly, to the girl's apartment ... there the man said goodbye, the girl ran into the house, I waited a while until she came out again, and then we went to a hotel. ... Even before we got to the hotel all this was charming, exciting, and horrible, in the hotel it wasn't different.[16]

Kafka's anecdote condenses the melancholy nature of modern love which is not love.

Has the geography of the postmodern changed all that? On the Los Angeles freeways men and women behind the wheels of their automobiles signal their desires to one another as they stream past on the roads enlaced like ribbons in the polluted haze of an eternal summer. Is that a heightening of the romantic effect or a zone of Reichian disinhibition?

In his letters Kafka inhabits an emotional world which resembles that of the Surrealists. They sought 'profane illumination', sometimes in drugs, but more importantly in the unexpected juxtapositions and even the deadly monotony of the everyday. They sought it also in explorations of the unconscious; and in love. What was important, for the Surrealists – and for the twelfth-century poets of courtly love, who also interested them[17] – was more than sensual pleasure, it was an intensity that would illuminate the world.

Something of this is sought, too, in the postmodern search for the 'sublime', for the intoxication of fragmentation and the dissolving of the barriers between the real and the unreal, and in the way in which all postmodern experience is aestheticized, euphoric yet horror-stricken. Milena Jesenska, Kafka's last love, 'you who live your life so intensely down to such depths,' as he wrote, seems to have lived her life in search of 'profane illumination'. It is as yet unclear what will be the result for romantic love of women's irruption into the theatre of love as active participants instead of the mere objects of love that they were for the Surrealists as much as for Stendhal.

And Felice Bauer? Who knows what Felice Bauer desired.

19

No More Remission

'Henceforth there would be no discontinuity, no gap, no dead time, no remission.'

The Story of O

It was January, yet spring, summer and autumn bloomed together. I walked through empty suburbs. There was no sidewalk for pedestrians. From time to time a car cruised round a bend in the road, endangering me, but quietly. Olive trees grew along the verge, and the fruit littered the tarmac, staining it a purplish black where the olives had been crushed by tyre treads. Fluffy tails of bright yellow mimosa plunged downwards out of a grey froth of leaves. A shrub glared with autumn red. I saw no one, the territory was deserted. The single storey houses were set back in blinkered privacy beyond their squares of lawn, vacant, impenetrable. A drugged peace sealed this two-dimensional world.

Would it be safe to walk here at night? They always told you how dangerous everywhere was. And then, there had been a murder –

The flat campus opened unexpectedly in front of me. Agoraphobic in the giddying light of it, I walked towards the biscuit-coloured buildings, which rose pale and Edwardian in the middle distance.

The chapel was in the central quad. They'd found a woman's body – oh, several years ago. Her throat was slit. It was an unsolved crime, they never found out who or why.

I crossed the quad with its central tangle of palms and monkey puzzle trees. It was awhir with bicycles. It reminded me of Cambridge – except for the students. They were uniformly tanned, they smiled indistinguishably, blank smiles, like Midwich cuckoos from another planet. Aliens concealed in human form, free of the blemish of human contradiction, they gazed inscrutably at the world.

The chapel doors were heavy to pull open. Inside, yellow light fell on gilded mouldings and garish murals. Intrusive objects – lecterns, pews, tables – filled the small space and a suffocating silence reminded me of what always seems so clear in such places: that the palpable absence of god is itself a presence, thick, malevolent, annihilating.

Had she been murdered here, dragged here, lured, was she at prayer, or was it an illicit rendezvous, or even something political? Maybe they just dumped the body afterwards.

I came out of the oily gloom into the radiance of the quad, walked through the arched cloister and out onto the wide, white stone steps. They led down to the loop that terminated the driveway. I stared along the endless road to the point at which it vanished between its lines of palms, a pinpoint far away in a shimmering dissolve.

Trees of California: squat palms with giant unfurling leaves and pineapple trunks; tall giraffes' tails with a single tuft of leaves. Beyond them herded the eucalyptus, sweeping the ground from a hundred feet up with filmy shoals of leaves.

For the first time in my life I was completely alone. Now, there would be rain along the Weteringschans, the canal water would swill between its walls like tea, the buildings would be veiled in mist as the trams rattled past, while behind the high windows with their thick lace curtains and their plants the orange light invited you to a winter teatime. Or you could drink Genever in a bar with turkey carpets on the tables and men in seamen's clothing leaning against the wooden counter. A feeling of homesickness – only . . . *he* was there. So the feeling died, irradiated in the hot sun and the blue sky, frizzled to nothingness in a landscape indifferent to feeling.

Every day I walked through the deserted suburbs, road after road curving between my apartment and the campus. The brilliant flowers and berries sprang together from the trees, fuchsia, yellow, orange against the dark evergreens and pale spring leaves. The place was like an alien, transformed Kew Gardens. The lawns were greener, even, than you would see in England – yet it was all an illusion. At every corner on every road the mechanical sprinklers clicked and nodded to and fro to create it. But underneath the astroturf the place was a desert. Underneath the mirage there was nothing but the bog oaks and rattlesnakes of a hundred years ago. They were only waiting; one day they would come back. Their moment would come after the nuclear disaster, or after the earthquake. There were instructions about the earthquake – in my apartment, in the faculty office, all over the campus. An event foretold, expected, certain – yet not real: blank smiles.

In the mornings steam curled off the hot tub next to the pool. The sun rose quickly, piercing the apartment, which had windows on all sides. Yet however early I was up, there were always others before me: a jogger, a cyclist, the paper boy, the mother with her newborn baby. The men left for work, also early; the faculty wives stayed behind, piled the toddlers into their cars, while groups of older children ran across the lawns. In the early evenings they held drinks parties behind the identical picture windows with identical drapes. No one walked out after dark, there was only the soft purr of the cars.

I walked across the open-plan and stared out of the windows on the other side, at the line of lights like stars against the black highway, and at a more distant glimmer of lights on the far side of the bay. An ancient memory swam up: I'm looking out of a window at night and lights prick out some distant city on the horizon far away, an image of adult life, exciting and out of reach.

Other times, early evenings with a chill coming off the valley and the fog rolling across the bay I thought of the Weteringschans again, of the tram clanging along the Overtoom and the high, secluded houses behind the Von-delpark and I wondered if *he* were still in the attic room,

154

one hundred and twenty-four stairs to that room. . . . So often it rained, there – a watery city, not like this dry land; rather, the intimacy, the reassurance of the blue damp of melancholy evenings in that northern city moored, floating against the continent of Europe, warrened as a coral reef, tunnelled with sea water.

Until now I'd known only the rooms, the interiors of the East coast; like Europe those northern cities, built of stone and brick – they used to remind me of Amsterdam. Out here, it was different. The low buildings, which looked like Japanese houses, might turn out to be computer factories, schools, clinics, anything. Profusion of façades – Spanish, Japanese, Western, there was no correspondence to function; architecture, like the seasons, was confused. And like what I saw in the papers, the sexual abuse of children, the confusion flowed everywhere, a dark undertow, but tacky too: the breakdown of the generational divide, of distinctions in architecture, the confusion of seasons: there was no established set of meanings, and hence the blank smiles, they were just masks of normality to hide that confusion.

Still, I'd escaped, I was safe, becalmed on the shore of the Pacific Ocean. I'm here at last, I thought, as the taxi slid down the ramp road that looped towards the freeway from San Francisco airport. But this was not San Francisco: this was a flat wasteland, a swamp planted with hotels and palms; for miles we rolled past gas stations and burger joints, cottage shops and Spanish shopping malls. Later they told me the airport was built on land that didn't even exist in the fifties, sludge dredged up from the bottom of the bay. Apricots and peaches grew along the valley in the fifties; now it was like trench warfare, stumps sticking out of mud along the shoreline, and only the drifters and the old and the Mexicans ride the buses along the El Camino. And all down the valley from San Francisco to San José, down through the middle-class shanty towns of Redwood City, San Mateo, Burlingame, all you can do is shop, buy.

Still, at least I was safe here, invisible. In fact, I had disappeared in this white abyss of sunlight, I barely existed at all. My new acquaintances stood beyond the glass pane of light that shuttered me into the silence of total calm.

And the ones I came to know were not real Californians, but chose to remain grittily New York, Boston or Minnesota.

'I hate this California sunshine.'

'I *loathe* the valley.'

But the Californians loved the valley. Even San Francisco was darkly dangerous to them, for all that the hilly streets glittered with the reassuring brilliance of a Brighton or Torquay, while its stucco, seaside suburbs dreamed in backwaters shaded by Ilex and umbrella pines, full of secret lives and idle mysteries. How remote now seemed the layers and layers of that old, brown city sedimented with centuries like the varnish on a Rembrandt.

Once, I'd longed to be in San Francisco, I had a lover once from there – wrote me letters about the Beats, North Beach, the Hungry Eye café, the poetry readings and jazz. Now it's years too late, it's no longer there, it's gone forever, San Francisco of my dreams, smokey and existentialist and avant garde.

Hotter every day. I walked across the gardens, heard voices from the pool and a splash, crested the hill, now covered with lupins in a haze of mauve, and walked through the suburban roads where everything bloomed. Camellias and roses cast a heavy scent across the path. Then I reached the campus: alone in a golden universe. The pale tower gleamed in the distance against Venetian blue. The campus lay flat and white as wheat, opening out on either side of me as I walked alone towards the fantasy castle of learning, which floated at the horizon, with beyond it the bunched eucalyptus, their long tongues languishing in the heat.

I walked on past the library, crossed the lawn and stood between the lofty, peeling tree trunks in a tent of dipped branches. Beyond the speckled shade the light pulsed: still, white radiance. I stood, flooded with bliss, suddenly in love. The world changed utterly, yes, like falling in love, I was flooded with radiance: I was alive. How long did I stand there, blotted into the heat, dissolving into the camouflage of leaves, shimmering like the horizon trembles on a hot day, giddy, dissolving?

And then across the radiance of the day a thumb smeared dirt, filth.

Even as I felt the thickness of the envelope, stared at the European stamp and the pointed writing, I *knew* ... I'd quite liked him at first, but it was nothing special, he meant nothing to me.

Pages of it – a horrible letter. Pages of it, sex, sex, sexual love in unremitting detail, a menace, a threat, he was coming to visit me –

I stuffed it down into the trashcan, trying to get rid of the words that had smeared across the day. I'd been so careful not to leave my address ... I kept remembering those words, those suggestions – a violation –

At night the apartment was too open. Only a flimsy catch secured the French window at each end. I lay awake, tense, listening, expecting steps outside the window, the heavy shadow of a stranger through the thin curtains. Anyone could climb up from the highway, and cross the stretch of grass and shrub that rose towards the unprotected complex.

Sometimes I even forgot to lock the windows at night. I'd draw the sliding glass doors together and forget that I hadn't locked them.

I lay awake and listened. I had been asleep, but now I was awake. If you lie awake long enough in the silence of the night – *dead* silence – you always hear a noise. And now there was a noise. Shsh – shsh – shsh – like someone brushing the parquet floor with a stiff brush. It was just outside the bedroom door. Someone was crouched there, brush, brush, brushing.

I walked through the empty rooms in the clinging grey half light. There was no one there, but empty rooms are menacing, for there is always the shadow beyond the next corner, the worst is always to come.

I looked out of the windows. The sprinklers' jets of water jerked from side to side with robotic precision in the darkness and a sharp, brushing, whirring sound. Independent of human agency, the electronic programme had set them in motion. I watched for a long time in the aquatic

157

dusk of the apartment, frightened, too frightened to move. Only a pane of glass between me and the world.

In the morning I sat on the patio and drank my coffee. The motors sparkled as they slipped along the highway. The drone of the engines came from very far away. No one ever walked on the highway. Yet now I did see a figure loitering along. He glanced up at the apartments on the hill – he seemed to be staring at me.

They walked the El Camino, the poor and dispossessed. Or rode the buses along the strip that leaked for mile after mile out of San Francisco.

At the edge of every great city is a zone that is neither city nor country, neither urban nor rural, but where each oozes into the other, where boundaries are blurred: zones of pollution and of the mingling of that which should be kept apart, appalling regions. In the Bay Area it is Silicon Valley, zone of poisoned water tables, of shanty towns and cultural sewage seeping across what was once a landscape, zone of toxic waste dumps, mutated birds and even deformed babies.

There is no form of travel that shields you from these blighted limbos, but air travel is worst, airports are always part of the war zone through which you are compelled to drive: so that the Great Moment – your first sight of the illustrious skyline, of the enchanted turrets and façades, be it Manhattan or Venice – is cancelled out by the horror of outer Queens or Mestre, forcing to your attention the unwelcome knowledge of that Other of great cities, the ringway, the no-man's land, the unpicturesque underside, the contingent ugliness of the beauty of metropolis.

But not contingent at all – on the contrary, as necessary as the architectural beauty it supports. And hence its infernal beauty, the pleasure you take in it all. The horror bewitches you, you can't take your eyes off it, you become an America junkie, drowned in the junk of the real America.

I loved the library. I climbed the carpeted stairs, walked between the stacks, my footsteps silenced by the deep pile, and found a corner by the window. I looked down on the

forecourt and watched the students wheeling and turning
their bikes in silent, mimed conviviality beyond the pane
of glass.

I almost lived here now. It seemed safer than the apartment. And really you need never go home. There were
alcoves furnished with coffee tables and sofas big enough
to sleep on, the lavatories were luxurious, and there were
even vending machines with coffee and snacks.

I read at random, picking books down from the shelves
of this de luxe hotel of learning. Best of all I liked the
American West collection: California – a place consciously
built as the embodiment of a dream, but on the foundations
of such violence and greed: the Gold Rush, so many
murders, so much drinking in the shebeens and brothels
along the Barbary Coast – men fighting in the mud, the
death of hopes; and yet within fifty years the gracious
communities were flowering on the rim of the Pacific, this
very university the dream of a new learning, a fusion of
European scholarship with the spirit of the New World;
the dream of a beautiful life, the Californian dream.

It grew hotter. I read. I was safe here, wasn't I, I'd
escaped. It was a refuge from the letters that came, that
said the same things over and over again. He'd even told
me what day he'd be arriving. This was my sanctuary.

I took the lift to the basement and came out into identical
red-carpeted corridors between high shelves. These were
even more deserted than those upstairs. They stretched
away into the twilight. No one was there – or if they were
no steps were heard on the velvet floor until, turning a
corner, you jumped at the sight of a silent figure right
beside you.

A slope led to an iron door and then into the hinterland
of the reserve stacks. This was a region, also deserted, of
concrete floors and rattling iron stairways and walkways.
Here, there was wary avoidance of any other prowling
stranger, intruders guiltily avoided human contact. Here
were no graduate students hanging out, their feet on the
sofas, chewing gum and gossiping in whispers, this was a
hardcore zone in which encounters were furtive, only the
really addicted readers came this far, to the back wards of

the palace of dreams. I hurried along the springing iron lattice-work of the walkways, giddily glancing down at the floor below and hurrying, hurrying –

I used to tell myself that I needn't open the mailbox, that I needn't open the letters.

'Soon I'll be with you . . . my flight will arrive –'

It was crazy of course. He hadn't any money –

I made a note of the date. I'd hole up in the city, get a flight to New York maybe –

I watched the red rapid sunset as I drank a glass of Californian wine. The Californians never drank, not the campus Californians anyway. I remembered the smokey bars along the canals, the evenings in my old, dim room high above the Weteringschans, where the trams rang and rattled along the street.

At night there were the shadows and the bars of lighter grey and glimmering pallor cobwebbing the empty rooms, a layered, fraught vacancy, the emptiness itself a presence, wakeful, watching, a crouching blankness that knew about my fears, about my longing to shrink into some space that would contain me, safe from the smear of that first awful letter, on that bleached-out day, with its dark stain that oozed across, spreading, spreading . . .

Sometimes I lingered on campus, there were always lectures and concerts, things to do. One evening I stayed too long after a film show, I couldn't bring myself to leave the lighted foyer, the little group that stood chatting.

I set off across the moonlit grass to walk the familiar route. The street lamps at the intersection were raw and bright, and cars hushed by along the driveway that ringed the inner campus. I walked forward with determination – there was only the stretch across the open campus that would be really lonely, before I reached the suburb on the far side.

I passed the tall palms at the second junction and reached the open stretch. But here the street lighting simply gave out. If I went any further it would be in total darkness. I stood for minutes, unable to go either forward or back. Either I was a coward or a fool; a fool to go forward, a coward to go back . . . to go forward, to meet the fear, the danger, not to stay cocooned in the cradle of the normal, the human, the everyday. The darkness opened its arms to me –

A professor I hadn't met called me up, invited me to lunch at the faculty club. He'd heard about my work, he said. A thick-set man with a dark beard, not a Californian, he too longs for the darkness and the cold back East, for the streets like solid corridors, for the gloomy northern cities like the Europe from which his grandparents came, not this packing case world, this world of sheds and cardboard palms.

'They do nothing here but work – you'd think at the pool at least they'd hang out, play the radio, but no: it's do your thirty laps and back to the library –'

I wondered if he liked me – if he'd invite me again. I thanked him for the lunch; he was non-committal.

Now the heat sharpens everything. I stare out from behind the drapes at the white, white glare. I'm restless, I'm waiting.

His car slides round the driveway. I recognize it from yesterday; dark green. He gets out with a small white package in his hand, which he places on the roof of the car while he locks up. He glances round. I'm not made up; my hair's a mess. But he makes off in the opposite direction, looking to left and right all the time, sidling, almost furtive.

Next morning his car's still there.

The semester's over. The campus is deserted. The students have melted away.

I went onto campus; no one about. I walked across the quad and past the chapel, and remembered that first day, the unfinished story I'd been told. But that's so long ago. There's only one last thing to do now.

In the red sunset I began the long walk to the bus-stop, cool in my cotton skirt and jacket. It's the desert air, it's a desert really, the night air is cold, even now.

I'd timed it well, I had to wait only a few minutes for the bus. Sometimes the buses were crowded, but not at

161

night. Only a couple of loose-limbed men, and a fat tourist encumbered with luggage en route for the airport.

Red and blue neon flashed in glowing streaks against the deepening darkness. I saw the lights across the bay, then the hotels, the planes coming in to land, and the bus drew up in the forecourt.

I walked into the crowded arrivals hall. On the board it said his flight was delayed: not due until after midnight now. Well, it didn't matter. I sat in the rustic coffee shoppe and drank weak coffee, ate cookies and waited. I loitered at the bookstand, went for a drink at the bar, but it had closed. I looked around. The hall was empty now – the place looked like it was about to shut down altogether. I sat alone, there was only a cleaner down the hall, and a woman at the check-in desk.

I went up to ask her what to do – she said I should go right down to the arrival lounge, where they get off the plane, she pointed me in the right direction. So I walked down this long, empty, tubular corridor alone. An empty airport seemed all wrong. Without the throngs, the crowds of people, it was eerie. I reached the end, turned left –

And came out into a little globe of warmth, for in the lounge stood groups of people meeting the plane, like me. There was laughter, someone had a can of beer, a girl ate an apple, it was like a party.

We saw the plane taxi down outside the window, close and huge. And then they started to come through, the voyagers. First in ones and twos, then more and more. I watched, I was trembling, my heart thudded in my throat as I searched through the throng for the familiar face. They crowded through, then straggled, the last one came and went. The door was shut. He hadn't come.

I ran back, along the corridor, as the last arrivals disappeared ahead of me. The airport was closing down for the night. I shivered; no cars, no buses, no taxi in sight.

He hadn't come. The surge of relief. But then – he must have come on an earlier plane, or else he'd have let me know, there must have been a mistake about the times, we'd passed each other on the El Camino, I'd never said I'd meet him after all, I'd never answered his letters.

162

I thought he must be waiting for me now, at the apartment. I glanced all round the absolutely empty forecourt. It should have been bustling, busy with travellers, arrivals and departures, greetings and farewells. But it was empty and silent and windy. No taxi would come. And anyway, how could I go back there, to where he was waiting in the cobwebby darkness of an empty apartment . . .

I began to walk towards the loop that spiralled down towards the wasteland between the airport and the hotels and the freeway. It was very windy now, and the lights were very acid, very raw.

20

The Cabinet of Doctor Caligari

'This, then, was the complete game – disappearance and return.'

Sigmund Freud

Freud has been reborn not as the scientist, but as the cinéaste of the unconscious. Today's Freud, *fin de siècle* Freud, is not like mid-twentieth-century Freud. He is no longer a psychiatrist, but has become a literary figure. Even in the early 1960s debate still raged as to whether his work was scientific or not. Now – who cares; that controversy seems prehistoric.

In a recent work,[1] a book of essays all of which are critical examinations of the case history of 'Dora',[2] the majority are written by women, and demonstrate the inadequacies, from a feminist point of view, of Freud's analysis of the case. They perceive these inadequacies, however, from within the broad, basic assumptions of psychoanalysis, seeking to extend these rather than disrupt them entirely. The most radical essay, however, by Steven Marcus,[3] claims that Freud is not so much a revolutionary scientist or even a great thinker as a great *writer*: 'Like other masterpieces of literature or the arts, these works seem to possess certain trans-historical qualities.'

To treat 'Dora' as though she were a fictional character, as Marcus does, is to treat the text in a 'postmodern' way, by dissolving the boundaries between the real and the fictional, as though it made no difference that there was a 'real' Ida Bauer of whose analysis the Dora case was an account. That, though, is perhaps precisely the point

164

Marcus makes: that Dora, as analysed by Freud *becomes* fictional, or that Freud's interpretation of her life, at any rate, is a fiction, an imaginative construction which throws more light on the period in which it was written and on the society in which it took place than on the girl who was its focus.

From this point of view, Freud's fiction is just of the kind most appreciated by the postmodern sensibility: fragmentary, arbitrary (at least on the surface), with a double narrator, and in which the plot has no simple, forward movement but rather tends to circle round the same repeated incidents. This is a surrealist fiction, or, as Steven Marcus argues, a modernist fiction, in which the status of the narrator himself is unstable and varying. Freud speaks with a modernist, 'unreliable' authorial voice.

Yet Freud's style of writing recalls another and different genre as well. Freud's voice is invariably that of the detached observer (although Steven Marcus forcefully disputes this claim). Freud is an observer to whom are attributed special skills that he himself modestly disclaims, emphasizing his fallibility and the fragmentary or uncertain nature of his solution to the puzzle that has been brought to him, or the unsuccessful outcome of the treatment. He cunningly presents himself with the appearance of hesitation: 'I must leave it to your judgment to decide . . .', 'I will not venture to judge. . . .' Yet it is this very apparent diffidence that places the reader in the position of an equal – a colleague, another professional, another bourgeois, another medical man. Just as the therapist makes a 'therapeutic alliance' with the rational part of the patient's ego, so Freud the writer makes an alliance of rational beings with the reader.

A similar alliance is made between the reader of certain kinds of thriller and the detective who narrates the story; or in the case of Sherlock Holmes, his confidant Watson can to some extent play a similar role. This alliance of sanity is necessary because the events to be related are horrifying, fantastic, in the case of Freud's essays and case histories, shocking. In that sense Freud is not quite a modernist narrator; his works belong to the epoch just prior to modernism, are within the tradition of naturalism, to which, paradoxically, ghost stories or thrillers could also be said in some sense to belong. In all these genres it is the stable male ego that sets a distance between ourselves as readers and the lurid, violent, sordid or uncanny events which, through the observer's lens, we are to witness. These stories of madness, violence, death, be they 'case histories' or 'thrillers', are contained for us – just – by the identity of the professional man, the scientific expert who acts as interpreter for us.

This narrator is positioned as representing the 'normality' from which the story deviates; without him, if the sequence of events were just a phantasmagoria without a centre, they might be unbelievable and would appear as meaningless as a dream. The 'modernist' or 'postmodernist' thriller, whose narrator is wholly 'unreliable' remains therefore a critic's pipedream, and works which have attempted to be postmodern in this way remain experimental fictions rather than detective stories.[4] The flawed or corrupt detective/narrator may add a twist of cynicism to the *noir* thriller, but disorientation must never take over completely. Indeed the popularity of the traditional thriller has grown alongside the development of the modernist, experimental novel, and the unreliable author has always remained a minority taste.

In the ghost stories of M.R. James we find a third kind of writing; it too closely resembles Freud's. James was only eight years younger than Freud, and wrote his stories during the period, from 1900 to 1920, that saw the production of many of Freud's most important works. James entitled his first volume of stories *Ghost Stories of an Antiquary*, and the musty odour of the antique certainly hangs about his narrator, who is even more detached than Freud the analyst. He is a dry-as-dust bachelor whose habitat is the British Museum, whose study is the past in its most obscure and bloodless manifestations. He presents himself as a rational, independent and objective witness who is simply reporting the fantastic events in which he sometimes participates but which he as often retells as second-hand. Like Freud, the Antiquary is never the 'hero', never at the centre of things, but always to one side, as is also the classic detective. Like Freud, he is the objective, but not the omniscient narrator; like Freud he is forced to master the incomprehensible events of the tale, always fragmentary, elusive, ambiguous, by the force of his intellect. Both are detectives of the psychic realm.

As a child I used to listen to these stories on the radio, presented by the 'Man in Black', Valentine Dyall. As narrated in his sepulchral voice I found them indescribably terrifying and have never forgotten the sheet that comes alive, the hand (W.W. Jacobs's *The Monkey's Paw*) that scrabbles about like a spider and strangles people all by itself, the painting that comes alive, the children without hearts who steal the hearts of the living, and the spiders 'plump as kittens' that creep in from the tree to kill their victims. These stories were truly uncanny, and every familiar corner of our austere and gloomy house was invaded by fear, by an intangible horror brought on by the feeling that one might 'see something'.

As Freud in his essay on 'The Uncanny'[5] tells us, one meaning of 'uncanny' is that it is the unveiling of something that should have remained hidden. Like the doll that comes alive – one of the examples in his essay – or like the 'monkey's paw' or the mezzotint, the uncanny has to do with uncertainty as to what is alive and what is dead.

In the city, waxworks, deserted museums, empty streets are sources or sites of the uncanny. It is precisely because there is 'nothing there' that fear comes to fill this vacuum.

I do not find it frightening to read M.R. James's ghost stories today. Their uncanniness is still there, but has faded to the mustiness of a cabinet of curiosities, a museum storeroom. They are bloodless – sexless too. Women hardly figure in them other than as housekeepers, off-stage wives, in one case a witch. Not only is there no account of love or lust, but even as motives these feelings are absent. In this sense they of course differ radically from Freud's case histories, but they resemble the dreams, symptoms and mundane events that Freud often narrates in the course of his expositions and before his elucidation of their hidden sexual meanings. It would certainly not be difficult to undertake a psychoanalytic investigation of the hidden sexual significance of James's ghost stories.

Not unexpectedly, Freud's analysis of the uncanny leads him to a sexual explanation: that the sensation of uncanniness is caused by the fear of castration. But clearly, from women's point of view this explanation is unsatisfactory, since, if this were the case, women would not experience any feeling of the uncanny, whereas actually they do.[6] To say this is not to deny that repressed sexual anxiety may be involved, particularly as uncanny sensations have to do with the emptiness of a space ('there's nothing there') where something, nevertheless, might be. But we could equally interpret this 'undecideability', this uncertainty between presence/absence as the unconscious conjuring up the ghost of the phallic mother; it does not have to be the horror of the castrated woman that is the haunting figure. A fear of women, of some threatening maternal figure may be involved; but it cannot be a fear peculiar to men or little boys.

The uncertainty about presence/absence is reminiscent of the child and his game with the cotton reel cited by Freud in 'Beyond the Pleasure Principle'.[7] The child had a cotton reel attached to a piece of string, and repeatedly threw the cotton reel out of sight over the side of his cot ('*fort*' – 'gone') and then pulled it back again into his possession ('*da*' – 'there'). By means of this game the eighteen-month-old child mastered the anxiety caused by his mother's temporary absences. For the very small child the mother's absence amounts to a fear of actual extinction, and the subject matter of ghost stories, and often of thrillers, is death; so it seems possible that an infantile fear of actual annihilation is at stake.[8] In the ghost story we play with and master our fear of death itself, just as the child denied the loss of his mother symbolically by throwing the cotton reel away and then drawing it back again. But the compulsion to repeat reminds us that these fears are never finally or completely conquered, but always return – the 'eternal recurrence'.

In 'The Uncanny' Freud summarizes his views on the repetition compulsion, as they were to be more fully expounded in 'Beyond the Pleasure Principle', which was written at the same period. In the latter work he investigates the problem of 'unpleasure' and the way in which human beings will not only endure but will positively seek out unpleasurable experiences, especially in aesthetic form. This touches upon the sense of disappointment I, at least, experience upon reading Freud's 'solution' to the mystery of the origins of the uncanny – and often, when reading his work, when the solution invariably turns out to be the dusty old machinery of the castration complex or some other familiar and overworked formulation, which creaks onto the stage with as much conviction as a pantomime horse. This disappointment, this sense of anticlimax resembles the equally invariable disappointment when the thriller is finished. You toss it away: oh, *that's* who did it then, I ought to have guessed, it was obvious – or, I'd never have guessed, how far-fetched. The explanation is always obscurely unsatisfactory, however imaginative. The expectation with which the reader is led onwards towards the ever-receding mystery constitutes the pleasure – of suspense – and the solution marks the end of the pleasure. The questions are haunting; the answers only ever ingenious, a mystery degenerates into a mere puzzle. Explanation destroys pleasure; anticlimax is the name of the game. The pleasure we take in these narratives – it is a form of compulsion – is in wanting them never to end while being drawn irresistibly towards the conclusion. It is not the intellectually coherent solution that gives us the pleasure. The ego may master the problem, but that is not what we really wanted; it was the leaking out of all that unconscious fantasy, the 'return of the repressed' that we desire.

The uncanny has a further, collective meaning. The constant motif of the ghost stories of M.R. James is the malice that reaches back from beyond the grave to touch the living. Invisible or half-visible Others dog the footsteps of their intended victims, runes traced on a sliver of paper have the power to kill, the pursued vanish into the mists forever, hunted down for having, however inadvertently, offended some spirit of the past, some unavenged and vengeful creature who cares not who it has so long as it has someone. In this respect ghost stories differ from the thriller, where retribution contains some lingering notion of justice.

Ghost stories are modern versions – archetypally, nineteenth-century versions – of old rural tales of evil spirits. As Freud says, a trace of animism remains in most of us (although he implicitly excludes himself) and it is as if when the agricultural workers moved in droves to the great new towns of the nineteenth century they brought with them their beliefs, their superstitions, the 'old religion', which lingered on in the urban corridor streets, the squares and dusty courts of city culture. Existentialist writers have explained the sensation of the uncanny in terms of the awesome absence, the spiritual vacuum left by the 'death of God'.[9] Christianity, which once acted as superego to hold back and master those more archaic forms of belief, has gone. So, in modern, secular culture these forgotten and indeed dead beliefs haunt us more than ever, becoming nameless, senseless, unanchored to any belief system, and therefore even more uncanny – because inexplicable. It is almost as if nature itself came to haunt us; it is the very absence of nature in the city itself which acts as the source for uncanny experiences and feelings of all kinds in the metropolis: empty city streets are always slightly uncanny because they ought to be crowded, noisy and bustling; museums, those cabinets of curiosities, hold the daily lives of the past in a frozen state, condemning the household articles and works of art of past epochs and other cultures to a living death; the artifice of the empty park is strange and horrid too; and little closed-in squares and shuttered houses take on an impersonal malevolence whereby we feel endangered by the very fact that 'there is nothing there'.

It is at the very moment when perhaps Western culture became finally and entirely cut off from nature – with the emergence of the great metropolis at the end of the nineteenth century – that these literary works appear. The disappearance of the last links between ourselves and nature brings on the nameless dread and the fear of death, which can never seem natural in the city and in the age of scientific progress.

Thus the uncanny is another side to the romantic longing and nostalgia for the rural past that arises with the modernity of the industrial age. The manic nature of city life disguises this from us – the crowds, the consumption, the perpetual excitement and delight. Which makes those wells of sudden emptiness and silence in the city's heart the more poignant, the more lost, the more uncanny.

21

Utopian Identities

'I have always prided myself on my ability to let my own life stand as one example of the road women take to feminism.'

Cora Kaplan

The identity of 'feminist' was always a problem for me. Not only the world at large, but also other feminists seemed to interpret it as a kind of character armour, unfractured by doubt or vulnerability. No chink in her armour for a feminist; she must be a heroine, a warrior woman, an inspiration to others. Moving between the twin poles of suffering and triumph which constituted the approved feminist path, she made the journey from victim to heroine.

I was neither. And besides, certainty for me had never resided in what I *was*, but in the ability to act. Initially the women's movement had opened up for me the possibility of liberation through action, a release from the introspection of identity. But gradually a new identity was imposed upon me, as alienating and oppressive as the old personas I had cast off. And this just at the same time as old problems, old uncertainties returned: the 'return of the repressed'.

Yet paradoxically in the hollow and alienated space between public feminism and private moodiness a former identity, of writer, was able to live again.

The women's movement erupted as a politics of experience: women burned to testify to what had been lost, silenced or never allowed to emerge into consciousness.

172

Directly experiental and personal writing was seen as political rather than as literary; indeed, there may have been a rejection of the whole conventional artistic enterprise as women seized on confessional writing as a way of giving consciousness-raising a more permanent form.

In the early writings of the women's movement women aimed to express the radical otherness of their experience, in testimonies that still mirrored the world, but which made it strange because their angle of vision was different. These were to be narratives of truth, and women were to bear witness to the authenticity of their lives, a hidden and neglected truth, but all the more subversive for that.

I'm not sure how deliberately the women's liberationists of the late 1960s and early 1970s chose or used genres that seemed to serve the purpose of speaking our oppression. In the beginning I suspect we just plunged in. But, since no beginning is ever completely new, the enterprise drew on and adapted existing forms: the political polemic and theoretical writing as well as experiential literature. Indeed theoretical and experiential writing have been for feminism two sides of the same coin, the one investigating the other. Raw experience is marshalled into intellectual coherence and given a pattern within feminist theory, while confessional writing rebels against the élitism and distance of academic discourse and returns women's experience to its immediacy. But neither would leave the other as it had been. The experience of women would operate to disclose the hollowness of the claims of academic theory to objectivity and neutrality, while theory would elucidate experience. This theoretical insight would then inform political action.

Yet the fact that the purpose was always political could lead to difficulties. Political writing is meant not only to change people's minds but also to change the world. Theory on the other hand may become an end in itself, leading further and further into the convoluted passages of the mind rather than onto the highways of the world, while the political message may flatten the complexity of our lived experience to the one-dimensional caricature I came to feel was imposed upon my own experience and which

173

can reduce dense, contradictory life to a pattern book for right-on women.

These difficulties have to do with the peculiar nature of women's place in society (whether this is defined as oppressive or not). It is clear that women are unequal to men, and not only that but their over-sexualized role can lead to a form of degradation. Yet at the same time the very inequality and degradation can seem to be rooted in what is fundamental to human life: the difference between men and women, a difference that is perceived and experienced as necessary, desirable, and indeed pleasurable.

Women's exploration of this contradictory position is therefore bound to be fraught with difficulty and it is bound to open up what Cora Kaplan calls 'the Pandora's box of female subjectivity'.[1] Pandora's box contained all the evils of the world, as well as hope, and women have found that the desire to politicize the personal is not easily fulfilled; to map political solutions onto this knotty, resistant, obdurate female subjectivity has led to a flood of writing and theorizing that has extended the maze of subjective experience rather than bringing us out of the wood and into the clear light of day on open ground. We still glimpse the shining horizons intermittently through a tangle of branches. The wide plains of non-contradictory existence seem just as far off however fast we travel. Like Alice through the Looking Glass.

But: 'It is better to travel hopefully than to arrive.' The journey itself has become the objective and women's writing has gradually changed.

An anthropologist, George Devereux, said that all research is really autobiographical. Certainly mine was. I wrote about the welfare state in order to try to make sense of my own frustrating and inauthentic experience as a social worker. I wrote about women in the 1950s, in what I thought of as a form of depersonalized autobiography, in order to dispel what I felt to be a feminist myth of the 1970s – that women were pushed back into the home after World War Two, that they were once more immured and restricted; when my memory of the 1950s was at least in part a sense of new possibilities, of the 'modern' as the key

174

to the ideology of that period, my memory the memory of a period that was forward, not backward looking.

I turned to explicitly autobiographical writing in order to interrogate what I experienced as a further set of distortions – the untruths of that feminist identity I had found forced upon me and which I found so oppressive; and which I felt was falsely celebrated in a particular feminist genre: feminist confessional writing. The feminist confession could almost become a formula: a childhood characterized by emotional neglect, poverty, often sexual abuse; a period as a wife and mother struggling with the recalcitrance of men and the social isolation of the housewife – the 'problem that has no name'; at length escape to a new world, through education, divorce or employment, or a combination of these; the discovery of feminism; finally recognition by the media and worldly success, together with in all likelihood the fulfilment of lesbian relationships.

This story is not so different from that narrated in the novels of the 'Angry Young Men' of 1950s Britain, who wrote of escape from the prison of working-class or lower middle-class life, rejecting the norms of respectability and deference, and the defeated hopes in which they saw their parents suffocated. Those writers, however, displayed a certain cynicism about the affluent bourgeois freedoms to which they nevertheless continued to aspire. Feminist confessional literature by contrast expressed utopian impulses; a wholly new consciousness, a transformed way of life is possible within the confines of the old. Or rather we can burst through the barriers of alienated consciousness and material oppression by what is truly a triumph of the will.

I hesitate, wondering if my description is a caricature, whether I am confusing the travesty of feminism produced by the mass media with self-stereotyping. There were many different stories; not all feminist writings had happy endings. Not all were triumphalist. But the Strong Woman – who often became an Iron Maiden – of feminism *was* created within as well as outside the women's movement, too often imposing a particular structure of experience and response, consigning other feelings, other lives, to the dustbin of the 'politically incorrect'. New silences replaced the old. What appeared at first as a revolutionary 'speaking out', 'finding a voice', or 'breaking silence' could prove to be something rather different.

In addition the confession usually remained, in a literary sense, a conservative or at least a traditional form, its realism barely questioned. Readers and writers alike appeared to assume that the testimony reflected 'truth' in a straightforward way. These were photographs of reality. At first there seemed no recognition that, like all representations, they were artfully constructed. And too many of the writers of the feminist confessional work understood their alienation and confusion as part of the false consciousness of the pre-feminist period, feminism then being offered as a solution to these oppressive states of being.

For example, two of the most successful pieces of confessional writing to come out of the European women's movement were Anja Meulenbelt's *The Shame is Over*, originally published in Holland in 1975, and Verena Stefan's *Shedding*, published in the same year in Germany (and described on the cover of the American edition as 'the bible of the German women's movement'). Both were best-sellers. Each charts the progress of a young woman against the background of the 'sexual liberation' of the early 1960s and the students' and women's movements of the late 1960s and early 1970s: a journey from a false self to a new feminist self. But I read *Shedding* in 1985 and by then it seemed an outdated text which revealed the ideologies of the women's movement as crude and unsatisfactory. The heroine-narrator moves through a series of relationships which correspond to her development as a feminist, from sexual subjection to autonomy. She has a black, then a white radical lover, sexual relations with both being depicted as heavy and humourless. Neither man even begins to understand the heroine's desire for self-determination. She in turn grants neither of them any authenticity. Women's oppression is for her the only 'truth', even racism being judged as insignificant by comparison, while left politics is a mere male masquerade.

The heroine moves forward to a lesbian relationship, but this also fails. The two women seem to feel no spontaneous sexual attraction for each other, and soon take refuge in the idea that their relationship is essentially maternal. However the ideology of motherhood is not explored, nor does there seem to be any awareness that the equation of lesbian with maternal feelings is a cliché of conservative psychoanalytic thought. There is a gap between the relationship described and the rhetoric of the period about 'women loving women', and the resulting effect is of dishonesty and equivocation. Ultimately the protagonist's acceptance of herself as an autonomous woman comes to imply a view of *all* relationships as constraining and restrictive; at the end of the book she is alone. Celibate solitude is implicitly advanced as the journey's end of the search for selfhood, an ending which is surprisingly similar to that of another best-seller about a young girl who comes to self-knowledge through the failures of her sexual relationships: Rosamund Lehmann's *Dusty Answer*, published in 1927:

She was going home again to be alone. She smiled, thinking suddenly that she might be considered an object for pity, so complete was her loneliness.
   One by one they had all gone from her. . . . She was rid at last of the weakness, the futile obsession of dependence on other people. She had nobody now except herself; and that was best.[2]

This is a recognizable moment in the life of many young *middle-class* women. They savour that moment of coming to adulthood and freedom from intimate relationships even more than young men, since family intimacy *is* often restrictive for women, and the moment of freedom usually brief. (Most young women from the working class never experience it at all, even today.) Solitude, however, can hardly be a *political* solution, or indeed a solution of any kind. This is to elevate a mood or a phase to a significance whose weight it cannot bear.

In Anja Meulenbelt's autobiography the heroine's development is again charted through sexual relationships, from traditional marriage, through 'sexual liberation', to lesbi-

177

anism. But Rosalind Coward has rightly pointed out that 'the centrality attributed to sexual consciousness has always been a potential problem in feminist novels for it seems to reproduce the dominant ways in which women are defined in this society – through their sexual relationships'.[3] Since, however, contemporary feminism has carried over from the culture at large the belief that our sexual being *is* the core of ourselves, that in which our identity most essentially resides, it would be difficult to avoid placing it at the centre of the feminist confession.

It must be that many women read *The Shame Is Over* and *Shedding* with an instant recognition of their own pain. Yet that very identification with the *problem* makes it difficult to draw back from the conclusion, or to take issue with the analysis, even if it is less satisfactory. Although these were counter-cultural works, they tended to substitute for dominant ideologies about women feminist truisms which acted in terms of closure rather than opening out and encouraging exploration of that which we cannot yet wholly understand.

Rosalind Coward argues that as the feminist novel/ autobiography has become more predictable it has lost all political edge, and that 'transparent' writing (realism) 'where the heroine just moves unanalytically through experiences, is much more likely to end up endorsing dominant ideologies than questioning them'. For her, both Rosie Boycott's *A Nice Girl Like Me* and Alison Fell's more serious autobiographical novel *Every Move You Make*, both published in 1984, are little more, at times, than counter-cultural Mills and Boon romances in which men 'find the heroine compellingly attractive', while she gains neither affirmation nor insight from these relationships, but simply heads towards breakdown for reasons neither she nor the reader understands. This can then be interpreted, Rosalind Coward argues, as a moral tale against the dangers of the 1970s counter-culture, with its half-baked notions of sexual experimentation and drug abuse. Yet Alison Fell's novel could alternatively be read as an attempt to get beyond the dimension of confessional writing that so offended me in my desire to explore ambiguity, vulnerability and 'wrong emotions': the imperative of affirmation, the ideological pressure to 'celebrate' womanhood and women's triumphs, the longing for the strong woman.

These women become 'role models', women on whom we should model ourselves. This is very dubious. The 'exemplary' life inevitably embodies values and assumptions that shouldn't and can't be made universal, as Margaret Walters and Mary Evans have pointed out in relation to Simone de Beauvoir:

It would seem that in its search for universal explanations, and definitions, of women's subordination, feminism is ... deeply attracted by the idea of a universal, trans-historical feminist: a feminist for all cultures and all political systems ...

To mythologise de Beauvoir is ... to diminish her. As a life-long champion of the Left, and of civil rights and liberties for women and minorities, she is one of the most eminent and courageous figures of the twentieth century; as a champion of 'freedom' or 'choice' for women, she becomes a manipulable symbol for many of those beliefs and ideologies within the West that diminish human freedom.[4]

At the worst the promotion of women writers as role models becomes confused with mere publicity and may turn into what Helen Taylor calls 'the most suspect kind of heroine worship', at which point we are in danger of forgetting that 'the problem for radical readers and critics is that the obsession with the author rather than the text has been rightly identified as a bourgeois preoccupation which has worked against women's interests'.[5]

In so far as the feminist confession-writer puts herself forward as the exceptional woman who paradoxically typifies the problems faced by a whole generation of women, she creates herself – even if unintentionally – as a star. The role of the star, according to Richard Dyer, is to represent in a condensed form certain of the irresolvable social conflicts in a society and to provide a 'solution' to them in ideology. S/he and audience together create a magical solution to insoluble difficulties, and 'these star-audience relationships are only an intensification of the conflicts

179

and exclusions experienced by everyone'.[6] That is to say, the conflicts may be *simultaneously* highlighted and smoothed over by the 'star' representation and this may also be the effect of some confessional writings: both to express and magically to solve dilemmas. This makes their challenge to the status quo at best partial.

The role model is a highly selective representation, and almost inevitably she will turn out to have feet of clay. Heroic qualities may be undercut by the heroine's further evolution. In 1985 Dutch lesbians were telling me: 'Oh – Anja Meulenbelt's relating to men again – she's "come out" as a heterosexual.' I heard these words spoken on separate occasions by different lesbians, but always with the same wry irony, as the new 'truth' appeared to annul the inspirational confession of a past decade. In fact, to elevate women to the status of heroine is to do both them and ourselves a serious, even a mutilating injustice. To demand of other women that they be wonderful on our behalf is to see them as abstractions, and is to deny something that Anja Meulenbelt herself identified as important: the right to try new identities, new ways of living and new politics – and to *fail*. The certainties of affirmation are always only half-truths.

It has been pointed out[7] that the need to 'affirm' and the 'realism' of confessional texts at times combined to create the feminist equivalent of 'socialist realism'. In the Soviet Union the question of the relevance of art to the vast majority of the population and its role in revolutionary struggle was of great importance, and socialist realism was intended to ensure its progressive role. However, it was liable to self-caricature, and at times under Stalin was very narrowly defined. Artists and writers were required to use traditional, non-experimental forms to express the triumphant truths of the revolution. Nothing was to be shown that was 'negative' or 'decadent', and it had to be stated in the simplest possible way because 'the masses' were not capable of understanding anything more difficult.

There is something equally patronizing or else rather self-indulgent about the feminist equivalent. Theory is too difficult for us, failure and conflict are too painful; we must have utopia, that is, a non-existent place where everything is perfect. 'News from Nowhere' must always be good news. This is like Soviet defensiveness, which felt that to admit to any failure was to be defeatist, to betray weakness. So, for a woman, it can come to be defined as counter-revolutionary to admit to wrong thoughts or desires, to be anything less than a heroine.

Yet if the feminist confessional assumes transparent realism, feminist theory by contrast has made no such assumption; on the contrary, the feminist theoretical investigation of subjective experience has sometimes courted obscurity, and readers (usually other women) have sometimes felt alienated by an abstraction deemed to be unnecessarily obscure. The accusation of a wilful obscurantism has in particular frequently been levelled – paradoxically – at psychoanalytic feminist writing; paradoxically, because psychoanalysis more than any other theory explicitly incorporates autobiography and memory within its theoretical discourse, while its object is the exploration of identity.

Psychoanalysis introduced a whole new dimension to the concept of confession. It did much more than simply unveil the past, uncovering the 'truth'. It explored the way in which the recollection of the past involves a constant reworking of the notion of 'self'. The recall of the past, its dredging up from the unconscious and into memory is not a simple process of recall, but is rather the creation of something new.[8] It is rather as when jewellery or silver is dredged from some treasure trove at the bottom of the sea after centuries; eroded, encrusted with barnacles the precious objects have undergone a 'sea change'.

Autobiography then becomes simultaneously an interrogation of and the construction of identity. It can no longer be the telling of a straightforward story, the revealing of a pre-existent self, a person who was there from the beginning, a recall of the past 'as it was'. Realism ceases to be the presentation of 'the truth', and turns out to be just another style, another way of creating an effect. And Freud's work coincided with the abandonment of realism in many branches of art (although also with the beginnings

181

of film, most dream-like, yet most 'real' of all art forms). Art in a new, 'modernist' guise questioned its own construction, questioned its own representations of reality, and the deconstruction of appearances raised questions, as did also Freud's work, about the coherence of author, hero, self. Once autobiography had been seen as a source of truth, and the autobiographical author as an example to be followed; now, autobiography has come to be seen as another literary genre.

Although, therefore, the Strong Woman or heroic role model has always been seductive to contemporary feminism, there are other feminist writings which challenge it. At the same time, experiential writing has been used to challenge the abstract norms of academic discourse. Feminists have questioned the language, the form, and the content of writing. In the early 1970s Sheila Rowbotham in *Woman's Consciousness, Man's World* tried to connect her own experience as a girl growing up in the 1950s to her Marxist-feminist analysis of women's lives under capitalism. A new language is needed:

Our oppression is ... internalised. ... It is not just a question of being outside existing language. We can never hope to enter and change it from inside. We can't just occupy existing words. We have to change the meanings of words before we take them over. ... The exclusion of women from all existing language demonstrates our profound alienation from any culture which can generalise itself.[9]

After writing *Sexual Politics*, one of the earliest and most widely read theoretical texts of the women's movement, Kate Millett rejected academic discourse. In the introduction to her next book, *The Prostitution Papers*, she contrasted academic writing with the new style she had developed:

I no longer clung to that bleak pretence of objectivity routinely required of PhD candidates. ... My language had to reflect the experience itself; colloquial, excited, immediate ... I was writing at last out of direct emotional involvement. I began to write the way I talk and feel.[10]

Kate Millett was also one of the first of the contemporary feminists to look to confessional writing as a way of getting at troublesome female subjectivity, although she rejected the idea of confession for its suggestion of 'owning up' to something shameful. She believed that 'the shame is over' (the title of Anja Meulenbelt's book is in fact this quotation from Kate Millett). As Linda Anderson puts it:

What Kate Millett experienced as published author was an inability to reconcile inner and outer experience. The publicity not only destroyed her privacy but ... seemed to negate her own inner experience ... Both [*Flying* and *Sita*] seem both to chart a process of near breakdown and also to defend Millett against it.[11]

Kate Millett acknowledged a debt to Doris Lessing's auto-biographical novel *The Golden Notebook*, which had been published in 1962, and which became an influential text for the American women's movement. Doris Lessing and Simone de Beauvoir are perhaps the great mothers (heroines in the most ambivalent sense) of white feminist writing. Both sustain a belief in the form of writing they have chosen as a form whereby they can bear witness to the truth. What lurks, for them, at the edge of this truth, as its Other, is madness, although each responds differently to it. Doris Lessing is prepared to endure the disintegration of identity it appears to involve; Simone de Beauvoir locates madness in other women – women who in her novel *The Mandarins* especially, are likely to attack the heroine (her alter ego) – while she maintains what seems like a fairly rigid persona as a shield against fragmentation and insanity. Both of these writers also engage with, yet finally reject psychoanalysis.

Today, madness as a threat to female identity seems, in literature at least, to have receded, although (as Carolyn Steedman pointed out in a review of Elaine Showalter's history of women and madness, *The Female Malady*) the latest chapter in this history is the phenomenon of many feminists undergoing therapy and analysis. Nor is it that there are fewer women psychiatric patients than there used to be. As a literary preoccupation, however, madness looms less large in a literature that has accepted fragmentation and which constantly questions its own boundaries and the boundaries of the self. The dichotomy of sanity and madness dissolves in this negation of literary and psychic divisions, just as it is no longer a question of false consciousness opposed to truth.

Today it increasingly also seems as if feminist writers are likely to reject outright the traditional division between 'academic' or 'critical' and 'creative' writing, writing novels and autobiographies as well as theory; they also construct texts that do not conform to one genre or another. Carolyn Steedman, for example, in *Landscape for a Good Woman*, uses fragments of autobiography and reminiscences of her mother as a kind of oral history and analytic recall by means of which she mounts a theoretical critique of a certain tradition of working-class history. The mother in her narrative rejects the identity of the warm, and indeed matriarchal, working-class 'Mum' celebrated in the British sociology of the 1950s. Instead she yearns for a New Look outfit, which becomes a symbolic representation of women's desire, as against the heroic imperatives of a sentimentalized working class. Laura Marcus[12] has perceptively pointed out that Carolyn Steedman does not question the concept of 'identity' in so many words, yet her book asserts individuality by means of a series of refusals of *identification*: the coldness between mother and daughter; the refusal to share an identity with middle-class feminists ('I . . . feel the painful familiar sense of exclusion from these stories of middle class little-girlhood and womanhood, envy of those who belong'); the refusal to affirm.

Even here, though, there remains a bedrock of authenticity. She questions the stereotypes of feminism and class-belonging in which a one-dimensional awareness of oppression both creates an identity – at once individual and collective – and absolves the subject from the guilt of alienated consciousness. Yet this refusal in turn absolves *her* from false consciousness; may in its turn become a 'correct' self-positioning.

In my own books, *Mirror Writing* and *Prisons of Glass*, I too implicitly questioned the authenticity that has been taken as the hallmark of feminist writing. These books were simultaneously autobiographical and fictional. They aimed *not* to have a heroine with whom the reader would identify. Both aimed to prioritize the inconsistent and fragmentary over the coherent. (Whether they were successful or not is another matter.) In them I attempted to investigate the clichés of oppression I wished to escape.

This involved a distancing from confessional material, and, since the hallmark of confessional writing is immediacy, sincerity, this distancing may seem too artificed, irony may seem to ill suit the material, or may coarsen into caricature or camp. There was something that jarred about all this – although caricature and camp are meant to jar and can be powerful expressions of refusal. Yet irony, mockery, refusal can undercut every position. And it may be that in my very rejection of a transparent authenticity I covertly claimed the higher truth of the postmodern flux of identity and the disintegration of reality. As much as the compulsion to affirm, this too could become a modish and apolitical substitute for the holding in tension of incompatible intuitions.

By which I mean: not only as individuals, but collectively and socially we feel a sense of cultural disintegration; like Stephen Spender's parents as he describes them in his autobiography, *Worlds Within Worlds:* an Edwardian couple circling in a waltz – even though the ballroom floor had fallen away they still carried on as if it were still there. 'Things can't go on like this,' we say, 'but stable conditions need by no means be pleasant conditions . . . to decline is no less stable, no more surprising, than to rise . . . there is only one limit beyond which things cannot go: annihilation.'[13] Walter Benjamin wrote these words in the period of the Weimar Republic. Today, once again, misery and euphoria dance wildly together. What the British spent on Christmas in 1987 would have wiped out the IMF debts of three 'third world' countries, yet there are seventeen million Britons living in poverty.

Jeering, jarring, camp irony; a Weimar response. The hysteria can fuse enjoyment, horror, disavowal. To write may aestheticize our sense of fragmentation or confusion. Yet, we women who write, why do we do it, we hardly know. Is it our privilege, our refuge? Perhaps by writing, especially in the experiential vein, we aestheticize our lives. We 'give style to our character',[14] live life as art. Perhaps we are experimenting with 'that most terrible drug – ourselves – which we take in solitude'.[15]

Perhaps, though, the drug, taken not in solitude but collectively, alters its properties. Or perhaps we are like the Surrealists, who also experimented with the drug of subjectivity, but who did so because they 'sought to win the energies of intoxication for the revolution'.[16] The retrieval of the past, or its reworking, then becomes a way out of its thrall (as in the psychoanalytic cure), a renewal of the self, as the painful manufacture of memories becomes an acceptance of the self or selves those memories then become. From these we can then perhaps fashion an identity that is fluid rather than fragmented. Change becomes a part of identity rather than its fracturing. We are then not forced to choose between an inauthentic past and transcendent future heroine, but may inhabit less exaggerated, less self-conscious, non-utopian identities.

22

Interlude

I The heritage we renounce

Any discussion of women's experiential literature should surely not have omitted all mention of what is probably the most significant literature to have appeared in the last fifteen years: the writing of black women. It is inspirational, and expresses a strong *collective* sense both of the sufferings and the triumphs of a race and the women of a race. As one critic has put it:

The Afro-American autobiographical statement as a form tends to be bereft of any excessive subjectivism and mindless egotism. Instead it presents the Afro-American as reflecting a much more impersonal condition, the autobiographical subject emerging as an almost random member of the group ... as a consequence [it] emerges as a public rather than a private gesture ... and superficial concerns about individual subject usually give way to the collective subjection of the group.[1]

It has chosen, therefore, a different path from the path of uncertain, postmodern identity that I was exploring.

I am reminded of a conversation with a black woman student, who said to me: 'I can see *nothing* good in British culture,' and went on to talk of her commitment to the identification with the alternative tradition of black culture, which was supportive and nurturant to her. I remember my uneasy, almost sycophantic yet envious agreement with her. The contrast between her identification with a vibrant cultural heritage and my painful and rejecting relationship with my own so deeply flawed parent culture depressed me.

It is not that it is not easy enough in one way to reject a repressive, backward-looking, degenerating culture. Yet that is insufficient, and can easily lead not simply to an honest acknowledgement of one's implication in a racist and exploitative heritage, but to actual self-hatred. It is not enough to dissociate ourselves from Britain's role in the world, formerly as an imperialist power and now as part of a neo-capitalist vanguard; it is not enough to endure Britain as an unbearable dystopia which we can only dream of leaving, as we sink into a twilight of empire that does curiously resemble the decline of Rome. (This was the comparison made by Lord Denning in 1960 to warn us of what would happen to Britain were women to become more emancipated; and by MPs and Members of the House of Lords in the debates of the same period on the Wolfenden Report, which recommended the decriminalization of male homosexuality.)

In this cultural climate it becomes more and more difficult to resist, since cynicism replaces belief. The bankrupt rhetoric of Labour party 'patriotism' will not do, an aping of right-wing views in the vain hope of magically giving them a progressive twist by appending to them the word 'socialism' (how empty a signifier in such circumstances). Yet Britain still plays a significant role in the world economy, and the struggle for alternative views in this country therefore remains important. Both cynicism and self-hatred represent only the other side of the coin to bigotry and repression. In the end a way through has to be found to new sources of political identification.

In his article 'The Heritage We Renounce'[2] Lenin argued (in the then existing circumstances in Tsarist Russia) for the development of a working-class identity and consciousness, as against the sentimentalized and false rural/peasant identity advocated by the Narodniks as a blueprint for the future. Although circumstances have changed, the problem is essentially the same.

The postmodern 'crisis' of identity, authority and politics is one way of representing the problem. Perhaps it is also in danger of aestheticizing a non-solution. Some would argue that that is not the case, and that postmodern culture offers a space for the emergence and coexistence of cultural Others. The alternative presented in the writings of black women treads a path that lies between the alternatives of postmodern uncertainty and the fundamentalist traditional identities to which some cultures, and some groups in the West have turned. This black women's voice is an extremely important one.

II A demonstration

I interrupted my revision of the last essay in this book in order to go on the march that was organized in protest against Clause 28 of the Local Government Bill, which would outlaw the 'promotion' of homosexuality. On a grey, bleak midday we assembled on the Embankment, near Waterloo Bridge. More and more men and women gathered in a side street, and at length the procession set off down the Strand.

Not for many years had I been on a march that was so little policed. Was this because a much smaller march had been anticipated, or was it because we were already seen as outside the law and therefore as no longer citizens worthy of protection?

In Whitehall the march spilled all over the road, and a group spontaneously broke away to stage a sit-down protest at the entrance to Downing Street. For nearly half-an-hour the demonstration milled all over the main thoroughfare. Buses came to a halt. The drivers leant against the wheel beneath the cab and smoked. There was a hiatus.

Eventually we moved on again, crossed Westminster Bridge and passed into the shabby regions of Vauxhall and Kennington. No one, apart from a few rather drunken men who surged out of a pub, displayed any hostility as we trudged our way to the little park beside the Imperial War Museum. By the time we reached the muddy green the sky was so overcast that I could not understand why it wasn't raining, until I realized that it was actually getting dark. We had been on the march for four hours.

As I listened to the speeches – and these were interrupted by warnings of arrests and heavy-handed treatment by the reinforcements of police, some mounted, that had at last caught up with the marchers – I wondered if this was not a postmodern occasion in itself: a moment when oppression is both real and intangible, a moment poised between democracy and fascism, when we have left one but have not quite entered the other, a moment that seems uncertain to us, the participants, now, whose meaning will be finally decided only by the future evolution of events.

23

Rewinding the Video

'Things fall apart; the centre cannot hold.'

William Shakespeare
Troilus and Cressida

The terms 'postmodernism' or 'the postmodern' are less precise categories than different versions of an all-embracing gesture which sums up a spirit of the times, an atmosphere. The terms none the less refer to a philosophical debate, to a debate about knowledge and history, to a debate within artistic and architectural fields, and to a political debate, and at times act to unite all these, perhaps misleadingly. The terms are associated with a variety of aesthetic practices and a range of political positions. And, of special importance, at least at the radical end of the debate, is the positioning of women. In a curious way 'women' seems to act as a form of connective tissue to draw these arguments together into a false coherence.

At the same time postmodernism expresses the *incoherence* of contemporary urban life in the upheaval of economic restructuring. The very townscape we knew so well changes before our eyes, making strange the familiar. Yet postmodernism claims to rehumanize the environment; its architectural mode is a sometimes fanciful, often eclectic mask of the approachable, and this aspect of the debate has reached a wide audience, in Britain at least, because Prince Charles has participated, throwing his weight behind the attack on modernist architecture and calling for buildings of human proportions. When he condemned the proposed extension of the National Gallery, the design that had been chosen was abandoned and a more 'traditional' one has taken its place. More recently the debate was renewed when he attacked the ugliness of the buildings surrounding St Paul's Cathedral. There are many who endorse his distaste for a modernism that has itself become conservative and conformist, in favour of the return to tradition that is hailed as an important part of the postmodern impulse. On the other hand there are those who criticize new buildings where a façade of traditionalism is imposed on undistinguished utilitarian edifices. Some, for example, have praised the new municipal centre at Hillingdon in outer London for an imaginative use of revivalism, others have pointed out that it merely imposes a façade of cottagey traditionalism on a structure which is little more than a very large barn. The appearances of the exterior have nothing to do with the structure as a whole. Similarly, a kitsch 'Palladianism' is sometimes used to front office or domestic buildings, but bears no relation to the ordering of the rooms within, whereas the eighteenth-century use of pediment and columns corresponded to the functioning of the internal space.

But if one version of the postmodern is the tasteful pink brick of the Sainsbury or Safeway superstore, there are other, more controversial postmodernisms. The new TVAM building in Camden Town, North London, a high tech postmodern building, was attacked as trashy and kitsch. A model of the building was displayed in an exhibition on 'Taste' at the Victoria and Albert Museum, as an example of postmodernist design. The designer, however, removed it, arguing that it was not an example of postmodern design at all. (In a rather postmodern way the exhibition organizers then replaced the model with a photograph and an account of the controversy.) Another, more local, controversy in Camden Town arose over the building of a Sainsbury's superstore: a folksy, low-rise affair was proposed on the site of a substantial example of 1930s modernist white-tile factory building. The protest did not succeed in saving the factory, but Sainsbury's has produced a high tech frontage to assuage the wounded feelings of the frustrated conservationists of modernism.

It was the horrors of the high-rise flat that turned popular opinion against modernism. The baneful influence of Le Corbusier was renounced after the massive demolitions of the 1950s and 1960s when tower blocks replaced slum terrace houses, and municipal architects have returned, humbled, to the cosy terrace house, the natural materials – wood and brick – the sloping roof and front garden. In fact the failings of inner-city public housing had as much to do with cheap materials and cut-price plans as with modernism, and Le Corbusier envisaged a total environment, not the housing estate for which he has taken so much blame.

But today the suburban ribbon development of semi-detached houses is rehabilitated, nostalgia casting a glow over *its* eclectic use of Art Deco, modernist, cottage and neo-Georgian motifs. In 1987 an exhibition in North London celebrated the suburb, and included a re-creation of the cramped suburban interior with its three-piece suite, and the 'labour saving' suburban kitchen, the dream prison of the 1930s housewife. Yet to some of its critics the postmodern impulse towards nostalgia – which also embraces the full-blown Edwardianism of Lutyens – represents not populist homeliness but a complacent and conservative world, in which domestic architecture built itself around a sentimental vision of the nuclear family.

Those on the other hand who favour postmodernism mount from it a critique of modernism, which, it is argued, fell for a dream of a scientific future based on the factory and mass production. Curiously enough, even in the dream home of the postwar suburb, domestic life was fashioned according to the imagery of industrialism: the home was to be a machine for living.

This domestic dream in the garden suburb was part of an utopian ideal that could be traced back to the late nineteenth century. One of the most influential books of that period was Edward Bellamy's *Looking Backward* in which he described a future world where slums, pollution and other evils of urban life had been abolished along with many of the oppressive aspects of domestic labour. Families had their own private rooms in restaurants, for example, and Bellamy devised elaborate systems for the transportation of cooked food to the home. Many feminists shared his belief that, just as domestic production had been collectivized in the factory, so the remaining forms of domestic labour, housework and cooking, would also be similarly rationalized. There were women architects, for example, who designed kitchenless homes in the early twentieth century.[1]

The utopia of William Morris, *News From Nowhere*, imagined a rather different world, in which design was to be based on the craft principles of the pre-machine age. He linked beauty of design to function and tradition, but he also wrote of the cleansing of the urban scene of its industrial squalor and poverty. A further utopian ideal was Ebenezer Howard's garden city. He too wrote an influential book, *Garden Cities of Tomorrow*, in which he set forth his solution to the problems of urban crime, poverty and disease. His new cities were to combine the scientific rationalism of futuristic planning with the traditional design of housing popular at the turn of the century. Architects and planners on both sides of the Atlantic were impressed by his ideas and attempted to put them into practice, but usually in the reduced form of the garden suburb. After the Second World War the British 'new towns' were a further attempt to put Howard's contradictory ideal into practice, and William Beveridge, planner of the postwar welfare state, was an enthusiastic disciple.

In all these utopias, however, imagined or actual, the subordinate position of women was to remain unchanged (the only exception being the work of some of the feminists). In the world that William Morris imagined, women were to remain the goddesses of hearth and home, although their status would be raised because their specific role would be more adequately valued. Bellamy had little to say about the position of women, almost the only feature of the future society which appears virtually unchanged. Similarly, in the postwar welfare state planned by Beveridge the symbolism of the home as machine or as factory positioned women in it more securely than ever; the wife and mother was the factory worker (or robot) in the factory home.

The architectural debates of the twentieth century have tended to take women's position in the domestic sphere for granted, and the contemporary debate on postmodernism simply perpetuates this, its protagonists having little to say about the specific relationship of women to either domestic or public architecture. Today, again, feminists alone have pointed out that the problems associated with high-rise dwellings – anomie, depression, child abuse and accidents in the home, and muggings and violence in the pointless open spaces and access decks of the 'slums in the sky' – apply particularly to women. The Matrix, a group of feminist architects, has recently commented[2] that although modernist architecture was once assumed to be socialist architecture, this assumption is no longer made. Women practitioners can therefore be engaged on the side of the postmodernists in so far as postmodernism is a new kind of radical project, not mere nostalgia for the past.

The alignment of modernism with socialism has become problematic in the wider debate, around postmodernism as part of a general critique of orthodox Left politics. It is argued that, just as modernist architecture became obsessed with an imagery of productivism and the machine, so Left politics was equally obsessed with production modernization and scientific advance, what Theodor Adorno called 'the philosophy of the workhouse'. The Marxist over-valuation of production, and one-sided emphasis on work was grounded, it is now said, in an evolutionary belief in an advancing civilization which was progressing towards an ultimate moment of truth and freedom. Marxism could hasten this progress because its analysis was scientific. The postmodernists, however, argue that this is a terroristic because totalizing and therefore totalitarian view. A totalizing view implies that all events are connected in the single march of history towards emancipation, a view that is now challenged, replaced by doubt and uncertainty and by an emphasis on the fragmentary and unconnected nature of experience. Moreover, it is argued, the overemphasis on productive labour necessarily marginalizes and excludes women, because women are outside productive labour, locked in the silence and invisibility of the sphere of reproduction: the domestic sphere.

Marxism is in any case outmoded because we have entered the 'post-industrial' period, are living in an 'information society' in which communications technology replaces the old heavy industries. The political consequence of this argument is a general questioning of the way in which, it is argued, Left-wing politics was always dominated by the notorious 'white male working class' (sometimes also characterized as middle-aged, as though women, blacks and the other 'marginalized' had the secret of eternal youth).

Two possible conclusions may be deduced from this analysis: either it is argued that there should be a wholesale abandonment of socialism or even of politics in general; or there is a call for the regeneration of the Left by the new vanguard of women/blacks/gays etc, although these are not characterized as a vanguard. Furthermore, we are gravely mistaken if we believe that Marxist thought bears any privileged relationship to the truth. On the contrary, Marx's theory and his theoretical and political project were totalitarian both in seeking to explain everything and in supporting the domination of all terrestrial life by 'man'.

Feminism can then be brought in as the major challenge to this Marxist imperialism of thought and politics. Craig Owens has written a controversial article in which he has pointed out that women have hardly figured in the debate around postmodernism, and he has attempted to integrate them within it. He recognizes that to position feminism as a critique of Marxism (which is in part what his article is about) does threaten to polarize the two, but argues that this danger arises largely because of Marxism's 'fundamentally patriarchal bias'. Yet there is a bitter irony in his perceiving feminism as primarily a critique of Marxism, when in fact it began as a devastating critique of *capitalism*. It is perhaps unfair to blame him for this emphasis, however, since it merely reflects the way in which feminist theory has tended to develop. The collapse of Marxism into little more than an instance of patriarchy, for example, is implicit in much feminist writing today. Craig Owens, too, argues that:

Marxism privileges the characteristically masculine activity of production as the *definitely human* activity (Marx: men 'begin to distinguish themselves from animals as soon as they begin to produce their means of subsistence'); women, historically consigned to the spheres of non-productive or reproductive labour, are thereby situated outside the society of male producers, in a state of nature.

And in a footnote he elaborates upon this statement;

One of the things that feminism has exposed is Marxism's scandalous blindness to sexual inequality ... Marxism's difficulty with feminism is not part of an ideological bias inherited from outside; rather, it is a structural effect of its privileging of production as the definitively human activity.[3]

These passages condense a number of vulgar errors surrounding the whole subject of Marxism and women, and of women's productive and reproductive role.

To look at it first from an empirical perspective, it is simply not correct to claim, from the perspective of women, either that the world is workless or that the industrial period is at an end; on the contrary, women are, worldwide, entering paid employment in ever greater numbers, although on increasingly disadvantaged terms, as part-time, low-paid workers, a highly vulnerable group. It is true that many of the new women workers are employed in the service sector, in fast food, retailing and cleaning, or, at a more affluent level, in financial and medical services, social work and advertising. Many, on the other hand, and this particularly applies to women workers in the so-called third world, are industrial workers of a very 'old' rather than a new kind; they work in the garment or electronic industries, where the conditions of the Victorian industrial revolution have been reproduced in a horrific way in the 'world market factories'. It is therefore inaccurate to talk of 'de-industrialization'. This is a slipshod usage to indicate the decline of heavy industry in the West.

197

And the 'information society' depends on the production of silicon chips, in which low-paid women play a crucial role. So the attack on a Marxist 'productivist' picture of the labour force is insular, marginalizing as it does those very marginalized groups – women and third world workers – whom it claims to be making visible. We may also question in this context the denunciation of Marxism as 'totalizing'. What we see today is the 'globalization' of the world economy – a totalizing capitalism. While our subjective experience of rapid economic change and upheaval may be disorientating, may seem to fragment our lives and to relativise all experience, an underlying rationality from the point of view of capital is clearly to be seen. Perhaps a 'totalizing' account of these developments *is* useful. We may have been premature to refuse a connection between economic development and changing ideologies. In the area of social welfare, for example, can it really be a coincidence that universal health and welfare services are under attack just as the economy is ceasing to have any use for the old kind of universal workforce?

The attack on trades unionism that tends to go along with the above critique of Marxism is also misconceived. Although it is true that many of the traditions of trades unionism in the West did tend towards or collude in the exclusion of women and blacks, the setting up of the straw man of the 'white male working class' blinds us to the always inconsistent practice of the labour movement, both in the past and today. There have been significant differences in the attitudes of different unions and at different periods towards women workers. There is also the important difference between the Left and Right wings of the labour movement.

In any case, to set up trades unionism as eternally and inescapably 'male' and as therefore opposed to the interests of women is falsely to homogenize both men and women. The problems women face at work will then incorrectly be seen as existing only in so far as they are women, when what is happening today, and not only in Britain, is that women are set up as the advance guard of a *general* attack on workers with the intention of creating a low-wage economy in which the vast majority of workers, regardless of sex, are employed on 'female' terms. Both sexes will suffer from de-regulation, de-unionization, so-called 'flexible' work practices, and men are already beginning to take part-time work in some areas.

Simultaneously, there is a small but (slowly) growing group of much better-paid professional or managerial women workers, and a growing gap between their experience and that of their exploited and underpaid sisters. The interests of low-paid workers of both sexes are therefore likely to draw closer together, while on the other hand it may be increasingly difficult to create a unity of 'all women', although there will continue to be areas such as health care and violence where their interests are more likely to coincide. But, in general, the vulnerable position of the vast majority of women in the workforce should be a reason to support trades unionism rather than to engage in the union-bashing which is such an unpleasant and reactionary aspect of the general retreat of the '1970s Left', and which reappears in the debate on postmodernism as an iconoclastic and therefore radical view, when in fact it is neither.

If, therefore, the feminist attack on Marxism is at least to some extent adrift empirically, it is also theoretically flawed. It is again inaccurate to say that Marx and Engels were 'scandalously blind' to the inequality of the sexes, although it is true that they did not foresee the forms this might take in the twentieth century. Nor is it correct to say that women have been everywhere consigned to non-productive or reproductive labour. This occurred in the West in the industrial period, but even there was never true for many working-class women. However, it was characteristic of the early writings of the contemporary women's movement to universalize this form of women's oppression. Western feminists reproduced, although unintentionally, important aspects of the world-view of nineteenth-century philosophers such as Hegel, Herbert Spencer, Charles Darwin and Freud, when in fact the situation which these thinkers sought to theorize and universalize was actually historically specific to the Western world at one stage of the industrial period only.[4] Contemporary feminists, like these nineteenth-century philosophers, tended to perceive the public and private spheres as separate. This schema was then mapped onto Marxism in a way that distorted Marx's conception of the circulation of capital and the roles played by consumption and reproduction. For Marx, production and reproduction absolutely were not separate; it was the bourgeois economists who so represented them. In the *Grundrisse* Marx argued that:

The aim is ... to present production ... as distinct from distribution etc., as encased in eternal natural laws independent of history, at which opportunity *bourgeois* relations are then quietly smuggled in as the inviolable natural laws on which society in the abstract is found.

In reality, however, neither can exist independently:

The important thing to emphasise is ... that, whether production and consumption are viewed as the activity of one or of many individuals, they appear in any case as moments of one process.[5]

Feminist criticisms of Marx as neglectful of the sphere of reproduction are therefore misplaced.

Strangely, this criticism of Marxist analysis as insufficiently all-embracing can be inconsistently coupled with an attack on the oppressiveness of 'its totalising ambitions, its claim to account for every form of social experience'.[6] This is particularly illogical given that psychoanalysis, for example, or for that matter feminism itself, are themselves 'totalizing regimes', yet appear perennially exempt from even the slightest whiff of reproach on this account. The vague, yet omnipresent concept of 'patriarchy' is one manifestation of feminist 'totalization'. It is derived from the work of the nineteenth-century sociologist, Max Weber. Despite extensive debate and much criticism it continues to be used by feminists, often as little more than a code word for male power or sexist behaviour. Rosa Lee, in a discussion of postmodern art and women, for example, uses it to refer simply to all male practices in the arts sphere. In general, in the discussion of aesthetic practices this patriarchy can be set against the pluralism of the postmodern. Here patriarchy comes close to being equated with modernism. Yet feminism, while complicit in a monolithic, and often highly deterministic theory of patriarchy, can simultaneously welcome the pluralism, eclecticism and bricolage of postmodern thought and practice, appearing heedless of the inconsistency.

The special relationship of women and postmodernism is an ambiguous one. It is argued that a politics and practice of the postmodern can grant women the place allegedly denied them in the dominant political discourse of the nineteenth and twentieth centuries. Yet writers note the absence of women as participants in the critical debate on postmodernism. On the other hand women's artistic and literary practices *have* figured importantly in the culture of the postmodern. Finally, feminist politics are often taken as absolutely central to the dispersal of that 'totalizing' Marxism whose phallocentric pretensions are in need of demolition. In all cases, women are positioned as the marginalized, the silenced, the Other. Postmodernist fragmentation alone, it seems, gives them a voice.

In theory at least, all feminist endeavour can then become postmodernism *avant la lettre*. Rosa Lee makes this claim explicitly:

Indeed, it could be said that the crisis of authority symptomatic of postmodernism has itself been instigated by feminist intervention within cultural practice and beyond.[7]

Yet she objects to male critics who, she alleges, have *reduced* feminism to postmodernism.

There are further inconsistencies in the way in which women's work within popular culture is brought into the debate. As we saw, the 'Left' politics of the postmodern tends to distance itself from trades unionism and the Western working class. In this it follows the thought of the Frankfurt School – of writers such as Theodor Adorno and Herbert Marcuse – and accepts their argument that the European and American masses are so thoroughly incorporated into capitalist society and so befuddled by consumerism and the 'culture industry' that they are no longer capable of playing a revolutionary role. Today this is expressed rather differently but the message remains the same: the 'white, male' working class is thoroughly reactionary – racist, sexist and materialistic.

Yet when it comes to the question of postmodernism and popular culture, the pro-postmodernists take issue with the élitism of Adorno, although his distaste for the culture of the masses was at least consistent with his general disdain for their political potential. Today, however, popular culture is seen as another challenge to the monolithic terrorism of modernism. Andreas Huyssen, for example, lines women up with regional, non-Western, black, and indeed working-class art, all of which, he claims, act as a critique of hermetic high art and high modernism:

It was especially the art, writing, film making and criticism of women and minority artists with their recuperation of buried and mutilated traditions, their emphasis on exploring forms of gender- and race-based subjectivity in aesthetic productions and experiences, and their refusal to be limited to standard canonisations, which added a whole new dimension to the critique of high modernism and to the emergence of alternative forms of culture . . .

Women's art, literature and criticism are an important part of the postmodern culture of the 1970s and 1980s and indeed a measure of the vitality of that culture. Actually, the suspicion is in order that the conservative turn of these past years has indeed something to do with the sociologically significant emergence of various forms of 'otherness' in the cultural sphere, all of which are perceived as a threat to the stability and sanctity of canon and tradition.[8]

Elspeth Probyn objects to this – as she sees it – appropriation of feminism by male critics. For, she suggests, in aligning women with other forms of 'low' culture, Huyssens does little more than set up anew the traditional dichotomy between high art/masculinity and low art/femininity, art (male) versus craft (female), and all the other oppositions whereby women are consigned to a sphere of emotional irrationality and their work judged as inferior.[9] This fear appears also to be part of the basis for Rosa Lee's objections to the article by Craig Owens. Angela McRobbie on the other hand, although also writing as a feminist, firmly links pop culture with the emergence of minority art from the black, gay, and women's cultures. Pastiche, parody and eclecticism are knowingly used, she argues, by these 'marginalized'. Like punk, such minority cultures have used the junk and refuse of Western culture to provide 'a vibrant critique rather than an inward-looking, secondhand aesthetic'.[10]

For Frances Spalding, too, postmodernism represents a crisis of authority in Western culture, and she suggests that women have done much to precipitate this crisis: 'feminist artists in particular have played a crucial part in the breakdown of the old order'. The postmodern women's art she describes rejects the modernist aesthetic of abstract and formal purism in favour of figurative art, and 'an interest in symbol, narrative and myth'. In bringing performance, photography and text, and politics, psychoanalysis and social context into their work, feminist artists have challenged the élitism of 'patriarchal culture', and have 'attempted to release the female image and female sexuality from male dominated conventions and the false identity that has been imposed on women'.[11]

This way of expressing it reproduces a common tendency within feminist theory to perceive a 'truth' about women lurking beneath the *false* patriarchal culture. Here then is a further inconsistency: postmodern criticism has questioned the Marxist concept of 'ideology' versus 'truth' as a theory that aggregates an unjustified privilege to itself, yet Frances Spalding's account of patriarchal culture reproduces the same contrast between truth and falsity together with the familiar notion of an ideology of the dominant culture as a kind of veil or covering over and suppression of the *real* truth 'underneath'.

Therefore, both those feminists who seek to place new feminist departures in the arts at the forefront of cultural experimentation, *and* male critics anxious to strengthen their defence of postmodernism do so by perpetuating a stereotype of woman as cultural Other, marginalized exile or speechless victim of a seamless patriarchy. There is no rent in the fabric of this male culture – until the advent of feminism. Then, feminism coincides with, or even *becomes* postmodernism.

In posing woman as always and forever Other, in perceiving femininity as merely the representation of masculine desire, and in lining women up as part of the opposition to the dominant culture and in particular to its 'male' rationalism, these writers themselves invent a totalitarian scenario which can never really account for women's resistance or ability to critique their own subordination. If theory and language are inescapably 'male', how are women ever to 'voice' their own marginality?

Craig Owens is aware that the tendency to 'totalize' is 'characteristic of all theoretical discourse, which is one reason why women frequently condemn it as phallocratic'. Yet he is also aware of some dangers here, and adds that what women reject is not theory itself, but the *male* tendency to maintain a distance between the person who does the theorizing and the objects of investigation, a distance that 'objectifies and masters'. For he is aware that anti-theoreticism can lead back to a traditional view of women as irrational, leaving men in possession of rational thought while women wallow in the emotional, biological and natural.

It is one thing for male intellectuals to interrogate their own practice, way of life and position in the social structure, the imperialism of their theory and their privilege as Western intellectuals – although it is tempting to recast their retreat into postmodern irrationalism as good old-fashioned false consciousness, the result of their alienation in the society of the commodity. But women have been systematically excluded from the domain of reason, so their demand for inclusion within it is one aspect of a demand for equality in general. Feminists have criticized Simone de Beauvoir's project of 'transcendence' – the appropriation of the male position – but it is unclear what alternative there is if we are to escape the role of irrational Other, the madwoman in the attic (or more likely in the cellar) of our culture.

Yet Simone de Beauvoir, despite her intellectualism, is largely responsible for our awareness of the concept of the Other, at least so far as women are concerned. Moreover, now that it has been taken up and given a more general application in the literature of postmodernism as a kind of sacred alternative to the destructiveness of the scientific mind, we have ceased to see its shortcomings. It has become instead a ghost in the discourse, haunting the reader with a sense of unfulfilled and shadowy possibilities.

The concept can be traced back to Hegel's master-slave dialectic. Self-consciousness, for Hegel,

involves an inevitable struggle between consciousnesses . . . it is the necessity of recognition that made sustained self-consciousness, for Hegel, inherently conflict-ridden . . . There can be no self-consciousness without consciousness of the Other.[12]

Woman is not in the position of a slave, for Hegel's master-slave dialectic is essentially 'a struggle between male consciousnesses'. This struggle is the 'story' of the emergence of individual self-consciousness. Women remain outside this drama; the struggle between men and women comes about as a struggle between the private and particular on the one hand, and the public and civic on the other. That is, Hegel accepts the nineteenth-century Western view which restricted women to the private sphere and then turned that into an aspect of their nature. The female, private realm is the realm of the family, of the particular, of the personal, whereas it is in the public domain, in which men operate, that the ethical life is developed and men go beyond the particular to the general. Hegel's account therefore universalizes the social practices of his own historical period.

Jean-Paul Sartre's version of the Hegelian opposition is organized around the activity of looking and the gaze. The Other appears as a paranoia-inducing threat to the autonomy of the individual's free consciousness. In any encounter there is always one who looks and one who is looked at. 'The Other is in principle "the One who looks at me".' There is anguish and shame in thus being deprived of one's freedom, one's transcendence, and fixed and lim-

205

ited by the look of the Other. The gaze of the Other is alienating and objectifying.

For Simone de Beauvoir, influenced as she was by Sartre's work, woman is always the looked-at, and in addition connives with this 'defeat'. This is an aspect of Sartrean 'bad faith' and in *The Second Sex* femininity becomes a masquerade that is the very enactment of bad faith. So far as woman's status is as the object of the look, the Other, this appears in *The Second Sex* to be closely related to the 'immanence', that is to the non-transcendence of the female body:

The female, to a greater extent that the male, is the prey of the species ... in maternity woman remained closely bound to her body, like an animal.[13]

This is not the Otherness that postmodernism has in mind.

Postmodernism, in claiming to undermine the imperialism of the culture from which it springs and in seeking to align feminism with itself to that end, urges us to wrest 'Otherness' from immanence and powerlessness and raise it as a Medusa head to petrify the Master culture. There is something suspect here. The rump of the 'New Left', which initially ignored or distrusted feminism, has, in the exhaustion of its own project clutched at feminism to repoliticize itself and to repudiate the accusations of conservatism, cynicism and cultural free-market yuppiedom that have been levelled against it. So, feminism has been hauled in to support every retreatist position: to discredit Marxism, to attack the labour movement, and indeed to abandon politics. In the process feminism becomes less a political project than a form of representational experimentation: one example, possibly, of the way in which postmodernism is held to involve a massive displacement of the political onto the aesthetic realm.[14] (Peter Bürger, on the other hand argues that 'the aim of the avant gardist protest is to reintegrate art into the praxis of life'[15] – art will change the world.)

And yet – the very imprecision of the concepts of postmodernism and the postmodern is exciting, even liberating. What it *does* achieve is to speak the atmosphere in which we are now living, an atmosphere frightening in its destructive vitality, disturbing in its iconoclasm, fraught with an eerie, because imprecise significance.

It is not actually the supernatural that we sense as we feel the ground breaking up under our feet. Nor is it an earthquake – a natural phenomenon. It is the upheaval of social and economic change, which takes unexpected forms and with unanticipated effects. Postmodern art and literature reinvent these juxtapositions in playful or disturbing forms rather than explaining them. Even the 'worst' and most degraded aspects of upheaval can be experienced and represented in what Frederic Jameson describes as a weird 'hallucinatory exhilaration' or 'euphoria'.[16] His word for this is 'schizophrenic', but the full experience of madness – so threatening in the work of Simone de Beauvoir – is absent from postmodernism. There can be no madness because there is no sanity.

Instead, the hallucinatory euphoria perversely elevates the most frightening aspects of disintegrating urban life into a utopia of our consciousness. We seize a peculiar beauty from the 'refuse of the phenomental world', explore aesthetically (a process parallel to the processes of psychoanalytic therapy) the most degraded, disavowed and ambiguous corners of our culture, hoping to turn up in these slimy zones of horror the real 'new' – or at least some clue to what is going on.

So, the postmodernist enterprise at one level sinks into a voyeurism devoid of moral meanings, and even into a complacent, because so complacently 'modern', reactionary stance – a stance that may even be tinged with fascism – yet it simultaneously expresses the horror of the indeterminacy of our experience. The anthropologist Mary Douglas equated indeterminacy – the absence of clear boundaries – with pollution.[17] Contemporary existence is inescapably polluted at every level. This pollution, the schlock and kitsch of the postmodern, what Frederic Jameson sees as the 'eclipse of nature itself' in the totally urbanized world, approaches the sublime in that it threatens to overwhelm us.

Thoroughly postmodern also is the loss of control, the vertigo we experience as the rule book of the political game is torn up, as the centre fails to hold. We are free to interpret this vertigo as the playful experience of a fairground of consumer culture, where the helter-skelter, the wheel of death, the big dipper or the whip offer us thrills without significant risk. Or we may see it as the eruption of the volcano, the rumbling of the earthquake. Or we may recognize it as the terrifying exhilaration of a new industrial revolution, when 'all that is solid melts into air'.

Like the characters on a video tape when it is rewound we are being hurtled backwards through doors, jerkily throwing up our hands (as in amazement or horror) and shooting off in the wrong direction in clockwork cars. The speeded-up, flickering imagery destroys the meaning that was previously taken for granted; once we've seen that we can play with the tape we are to that extent distanced from it. As we are in 'real life' hurtled backwards from the Postwar Consensus to Victorian Britain, from cosy democracy to some third world 'B movie' city, our first reaction is: 'this is not for real!' We never believed they could play the movie backwards. The reel unwinds, but we can't believe it's true, the smooth juxtapositions of the everyday are giddyingly made strange.

In *All That is Solid Melts into Air* Marshall Berman[18] celebrated the euphoria of capitalist disorientation – so vividly described by Marx – as a feature of modernism with radical potential. Currently, the postmodern aesthetic – and its moral agnosticism – recreates the disorientation. The globalization of information and media imagery dehistoricizes, decontextualizes our subjective consciousness of contemporary history; we experience instead a cacophony of narratives emanating from a multiplicity of sources. No single line of cause and effect could exist that could link all the disconnected happenings, 'stories', into a coherent discourse. We see 'everything', yet it means less and less.

This is a world devoid of values. Although 'radical postmodernism' implicitly sides with a collective underdog, this alignment is subjective and we are given no reasons why we should believe one thing rather than another; we might just as well go in for Erhardt Seminar Training as radical politics; Buddhism is as good as Bolshevism (or better); therapy replaces collective action; astrology is the name of the game. Indeed, the proliferation of popular fads suggests a culture in which all sets of beliefs sink to the status of subjective obsessions.

In this world 'Thatcherism' itself, for all the rhetoric of family values and a return to tradition, is the most postmodern phenomenon of all in its blatant inconsistency – the gap between rhetoric and reality – the emphasis on consumption, the presentation of delusionary euphoria. Thatcherism *denies* conflict, as does postmodernism itself. Postmodernism refuses to privilege any one perspective, and recognizes only difference, never inequality, only fragments, never conflict. It therefore clearly parts company with Marxism. With feminism also, if feminism is to be more than simply a representational practice. For while women may speak with all the voices under the sun, and unveil their invisibility in countless ways, a feminist politics must rest on a recognition that oppression, not mere otherness, determines women's existence, and that subjectivity is not simply an aesthetic standpoint, but is also the basis for demands for change.

We may celebrate the intensity of a world made strange, taste danger in a perverse reversal of values, find pleasure in playing with the tape, experience life as performance and play. Meanwhile the tape plays on; and this one they're not going to rewind.

24

Epilogue

May 1984. I saw *Venice Preserved* at the National Theatre.
My American companion couldn't understand why such
an obscure play should have been revived. To me it seemed
curiously apposite for the times, for postmodern times.

A wholly corrupt and incompetent regime is threatened
by a group of nihilistic conspirators. The two women, the
chaste and pure wife and the whore, are both passionate
and loving, but their passion and fidelity are useless. The
hero becomes involved in the conspiracy by reason of his
friendship with Pierre. Ian McKellan played Pierre, and
wrung every last ounce of homosexual feeling out of it.
Jaffier, the hero, however, betrays Pierre – induced to do
so by the pleadings of his wife. At the end the irrational
power of the state was symbolized by a great wheel that
descended and on which Pierre is to be broken, but, at his
request, Jaffier stabs him and then kills himself as well.
They die in each other's arms. It was like a Verdi opera
without the music.

'Sleep all day – Party all night – never get old – never die
– It's fun to be a vampire.'

Movie ad. 1988

Notes

1 Memoirs of an Anti-Heroine

1 Lahr, John (1980) *Prick Up Your Ears*, Harmondsworth: Penguin, p. 136.

7 Living Dolls

1 Freud, Sigmund 'The Uncanny', in *The Pelican Freud Library*, vol. 14, *Art and Literature*, Harmondsworth: Penguin.

8 Chic Thrills

1 Veblen, Thorstein (1957) *The Theory of The Leisure Class*, London: Allen & Unwin. (First published in 1899.)
2 Simmel, Georg (1971) 'On individuality and social forms', in *Selected Writings*, Donald N. Levine, ed. Chicago: Chicago University Press, p. 311.
3 Proust, Marcel (1981) *Remembrance of Things Past*, vol. 2, *Cities of the Plain*, pp. 641–2. (Originally published in 1922.)
4 Benstock, Shari (1987) *Women of the Left Bank: Paris, 1900–1940*, London: Virago, p. 48.
5 Ibid., p. 181.
6 Hall, Radclyffe (1982) *The Well of Loneliness*, London: Virago, pp. 324, 323. (Originally published in 1928.)
7 Ibid., p. 246.
8 Powell, Anthony (1960) *Casanova's Chinese Restaurant*, Heinemann, pp. 117–118.

9   Nestle, Joan (1984) 'The Fem Question', in Vance, Carole
    S. (ed.) (1984), *Pleasure and Danger: Exploring Female
    Sexuality*, London: Routledge & Kegan Paul, p. 233.
10 Krieger, Susan (1983) *The Mirror Dance: Identity in a
    Women's Community*, Philadelphia: Temple University
    Press, p. xv.
11 Nestle, Joan, 'The Fem Question', p. 232.
12 Rubin, Gayle (1984) 'Thinking Sex: Notes for a Radical
    Theory of the Politics of Sexuality', in Vance (1984).

10   The Counterfeit Detective

1   Moretti, Franco (1983) 'Clues', in *Signs Taken for Wonders*,
    London: Verso.
2   Chandler, Raymond (1979) *The High Window*, London:
    Pan, pp. 52–3. (Originally published in 1943.)

11   Modern Heroes

1   Salgado, Gamini, editor (1975) *Three Jacobean Tragedies*,
    Harmondsworth: Penguin.

12   Cabaret

1   Wright, Patrick (1985) 'The ghosting of the inner city',
    in *On Living in an Old Country: The National Past in
    Contemporary Britain*, London: Verso, pp. 228–9.
2   Moretti, Franco (1987) 'The spell of indecision', in *New
    Left Review*, No. 164, July/August, p. 28.

13 Money

1 Holtby, Winifred (1978) *Women and a Changing Civilisation*, Chicago: Cassandra Editions Academy Ltd, p. 148. (Originally published in 1935.)
2 Pahl, Ray (1985) 'The restructuring of capital, the local political economy and household work strategies', in Gregory, Derek, and Urry, John (eds) (1985) *Social Relations and Spatial Structures*, London: Macmillan.

14 Second-hand Films

1 Beauvoir, Simone de (1962) *Force of Circumstance*, Harmondsworth: Penguin, p. 138.
2 Fraser, Kennedy (1985) *The Fashionable Mind: Reflections on Fashion 1970–1982*, Boston: David R. Godine.
3 Dyer, Richard (1978) 'Resistance through charisma: Rita Hayworth and *Gilda*', in Kaplan, E. Ann (ed.) (1978) *Women in Film Noir*, London: British Film Institute, p. 93.
4 Ibid., p. 94.
5 Harvey, Sylvia (1978) 'Woman's place: the absent family of Film Noir', in Kaplan, E. Ann (ed.) (1978) *Women in Film Noir*.

15 How Much is it Worth?

1 Dyer, Richard (1976) 'Reading Fassbinder's sexual politics', in Rayns, Tony (ed.) (1976) *Fassbinder*, London: British Film Institute, p. 55.
2 Quoted in ibid., p. 54.
3 Crisp, Quentin (1978) *How to Have A Lifestyle*.
4 Jameson, Fredric (1984) 'Postmodernism, or the cultural logic of late capitalism', *New Left Review*, no. 146, July/August, p. 87.

16 Death City

1 Gledhill, Christine (1978) '*Klute*: 2 Feminism and *Klute*', in Kaplan, E. Ann (ed.) (1978), *Women in Film Noir*.

17 Not a Testimony

1 Shostakovich, Dmitri, quoted in English National Opera Company, *Lady MacBeth of Mtsensk*, programme, 1987.
2 Ibid.
3 Norris, Christopher (1981) 'Introduction', in Norris, Christopher, (ed.) (1981) *Shostakovich: The Man and His Music* London: Lawrence & Wishart, p. 8.
4 Kenyon, Nicholas (1987) 'Writing History', in the *Observer*, 22 November.
5 Norris, Christopher, 'Introduction', in Norris, Christopher (ed.) (1981) *Shostakovich*, p. 10.
6 Ang, Ien (1982) *Watching Dallas*, London: Methuen.
7 Endell, A. (1908) *Die Schönheit der grossen Stadt*, quoted in Lees, Andrew (1984) 'The metropolis and the intellectual', in Sutcliffe, Anthony, (ed.) (1984) *Metropolis 1890–1940* London: Mansell, p. 78.

18 Love

1 Kafka, Franz (1974) *Letters to Felice*, Harmondsworth: Penguin, p. 399.
2 Ibid. p. 429.
3 Ibid.
4 Ibid., editor's note, p. 100.
5 Proust, Marcel, *Remembrance of Things Past*, vol. 2, p. 134.
6 Freud, Sigmund (1977) 'On the universal tendency to debasement in the sphere of love', Pelican Freud Library, vol. 7, *On Sexuality*, p. 258. (Originally published in 1912.)
7 Kafka, Franz (1983) *Letters to Milena*, Harmondsworth: Penguin, pp. 141–2.

8 Stendhal (1975) *Love*, Harmondsworth: Penguin, p. 45.
9 Freud, Sigmund (1948) 'On narcissism: an introduction', *Collected Papers*, vol. IV, London: Hogarth Press and Institute of Psychoanalysis, p. 45.
10 Quoted in Jones, Ernest (1964) *The Life and Work of Sigmund Freud* edited and abridged by Lionel Trilling and Steven Marcus, Harmondsworth: Penguin, p. 473.
11 Gramsci, Antonio (1971) *Selections from the Prison Notebooks*, London: Lawrence & Wishart, p. 304.
12 Ibid., p. 296.
13 Quoted in Moi, Toril (1987) 'Introduction', *The Kristeva Reader*, Oxford: Basil Blackwell, p. 18.
14 Ibid. p. 239.
15 Flax, Jane (1987) 'Postmodernism and gender relations in feminist theory', in *Signs*, vol. 12, no. 4, Summer, p. 621.
16 Kafka, Franz (1983) *Letters to Milena*, p. 130.
17 See Benjamin, Walter (1979) 'Surrealism', in *One Way Street*, London: Verso, p. 228.

20 The Cabinet of Doctor Caligari

1 Bernheimer, Charles and Kahane, Claire (eds) (1985) *In Dora's Case: Freud – Hysteria – Feminism*, New York: Columbia University Press.
2 Freud, Sigmund (1977) 'Fragment of an analysis of a case of hysteria', in the Pelican Freud Library, Vol. 8, *Case Histories: 1*. (Originally published in 1905.)
3 Marcus, Steven (1985) 'Freud and Dora: story, history, case history', in Bernheimer, Charles and Kahane, Claire, (eds), *In Dora's Case*, p. 56.
4 Auster, Paul (1987) *The New York Trilogy*, London: Faber & Faber, is a recent example.
5 Freud, Sigmund (1985) 'Fragment of an analysis of a case of hysteria'.
6 *See* Modleski, Tania (1982) *Loving With a Vengeance: Mass-Produced Fantasies for Women*, London: Methuen, p. 31.
7 Freud, Sigmund (1984) 'Beyond the pleasure principle', in Pelican Freud Library, Vol. 11, *On Metapsychology*. (Originally published in 1920.)

8 This is the point of view put forward by Hélène Cixous (1973) *'La Fiction et ses fantomes: une lecture de l'Unheimliche de Freud'*, *Poétique*, 10; quoted in Jackson, Rosemary (1981) *Fantasy: The Literature of Subversion*, London: Methuen.

9 *See* Jackson, Rosemary, *Fantasy: The Literature of Subversion*.

21 Utopian Identities

1 Kaplan, Cora (1986) 'Pandora's box: subjectivity, class and sexuality in socialist feminist criticism', in *Sea Changes: Culture and Feminism*, London: Verso.

2 Lehmann, Rosamund (1982) *Dusty Answer*, Harmondsworth: Penguin, p. 302. (Originally published in 1927.)

3 Coward, Rosalind (1984) 'Cautionary Tales', in *New Socialist*, July/August, p. 47.

4 Evans, Mary (1986) 'A postscript on de Beauvoir', in *New Left Review* no. 159, September/October, p. 127. *See also* Walters, Margaret (1976) 'The rights and wrongs of women: Mary Wollstonecraft, Harriet Martineau, Simone de Beauvoir', in Mitchell, Juliet and Oakley, Ann (eds) (1976) *The Rights and Wrongs of Women*, Harmondsworth: Penguin.

5 Taylor, Helen (1986) 'The cult of the woman author', in *Women's Review*, no. 5, March, p. 40.

6 Dyer, Richard (1979) *Stars*, London: British Film Institute, p. 37.

7 I am unable to trace the source of this insight.

8 *See* Anderson, Linda (1986) 'At the threshold of the self: women and autobiography', in Monteith, Moira, (ed.) (1986) *Women's Writing: A Challenge to Theory*, Brighton: The Harvester Press.

9 Rowbotham, Sheila (1973) *Woman's Consciousness, Man's World*, Harmondsworth: Penguin, p. 33.

10 Millett, Kate (1973) *The Prostitution Papers*, London: Paladin, p. 10.

11 Anderson, Linda, 'At the threshold of the self', p. 64.

12 Marcus, Laura (1987) ' "Enough about you, let's talk about me": recent autobiographical writing', *New Formations* no. 1, Spring.

13 Benjamin, Walter, 'Surrealism', p. 54.
14 *See* Bellamy, Richard (1987) 'Postmodernism and the end of history', in *Theory Culture and Society*, Vol. 4, no. 4.
15 Benjamin, Walter, 'Surrealism', p. 237.
16 Ibid.

22 Interlude

1 Cudjoe, Selwyn R. (1985) 'Maya Angelou and the autobiographical statement' in Evans, Mair (ed.) (1985) *Black Women Writers*, London: Pluto Press, p. 20.
2 Lenin, V.I. (1977) 'The heritage we renounce', in Lenin, V.I. (1977) *Selected Works*, Vol. I, Moscow: Progress Publishers.

23 Rewinding the Video

1 Hayden, Dolores (1981) *The Grand Domestic Revolution: A History of Feminist Designs for American Homes, Neighbourhoods and Cities*, Cambridge, Mass.: MIT Press.
2 Cunningham, John (1988) 'The house that Jill built', *Guardian*, 6 January.
3 Owens, Craig (1983) 'The discourse of others: feminists and postmodernism', in Foster, Hal (1983) *The Anti-Aesthetic* Port Townsend, Washington: Bay Press, pp. 63, 79.
4 Rosaldo, M.Z. (1980) 'The uses and abuses of anthropology', *Signs*, Vol. 5, no. 3, Spring.
5 Marx, Karl (1973) *Grundrisse*, Harmondsworth: Penguin, pp. 87, 94.
6 Owens, Craig (1983) 'The discourse of others'.
7 Lee, Rosa (1987) 'Resisting amnesia: feminism, painting and postmodernism', *Feminist Review*, no. 26, Summer, p. 7.
8 Huyssen, Andreas (1984) 'Mapping the postmodern', in *New German Critique*, No. 33, Fall, pp. 27–8.
9 Probyn, Elspeth (1987) 'Bodies and anti-bodies: feminism and the postmodern', *Cultural Studies*, Vol. 1, no. 3, October.

10 McRobbie, Angela (1984) in *Postmodernism*, ICA.
11 Spalding, Frances (1986) 'Postmodernism: the new spirit in painting', *Women's Review*, September, p. 27.
12 Lloyd, Genevieve (1985) 'Masters, slaves and others', in Edgley, Roy and Osborne, Richard, (eds) (1985) *Radical Philosophy Reader*, pp. 299, 293. I am heavily reliant on Genevieve Lloyd's article in this section.
13 Quoted in ibid., p. 308.
14 Eagleton, Terry (1986) 'Capitalism, modernism and postmodernism' in Eagleton, Terry (1986) *Against The Grain: Essays 1975–1985*, London: Verso.
15 Bürger, Peter (1984) *Theory of the Avant Garde*, Minneapolis: University of Minnesota Press; and Manchester: Manchester University Press.
16 Jameson, Fredric (1984) 'Postmodernism'.
17 Douglas, Mary (1966) *Purity and Danger: An Analysis of Concepts of Pollution and Taboo*, Harmondsworth: Penguin.
18 Berman, Marshall (1983) *All That is Solid Melts into Air: The Experience of Modernity*, London: Verso.